MW00328841

To my dear friend, Steve:

Your suggestions have been remarkable.

Love,

Harrison

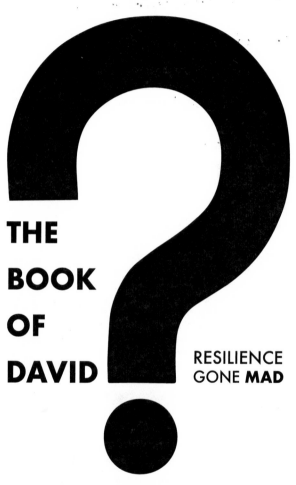

THE
BOOK
OF
DAVID

RESILIENCE
GONE **MAD**

A Memoir By
Harrison Rider Greene

Copyright © 2020 by Harrison R. Greene
All rights reserved. No part of this publication may be reproduced, distributed, or
transmitted in any form or by any means, including photocopying, recording, or other
electronic or mechanical methods, without the prior written permission of the published,
except in the case of brief quotations embodied in critical reviews and certain other
noncommercial uses permitted by copyright law. For permission requests, e-mail the publisher,
Subject: "Attention Permission Coordinator" at the email address below:

UniqueHRG @gmail.com

Publisher's Note: *The Book of David* is a memoir. It depicts events in my life and
the life of my son, David. Some of the character's names have been changed.

Special thanks to Harrison Demchick for editorial assistance and to
Claudia Greene and Ken Sayler for their encouragement and advice.

Cover design by Monique Muller

Printed and bound in the United States of America.

The Book of David/Harrison Rider Greene — 1st ed.

ISBN: 978-1-09835-702-3

For Claudia
She Taught Me Love

This memoir reflects the significant events
in my life and those of my son, David.

He became an addict who overcame obstacles
by deceiving himself that he was resilient.
I wrote it so that others might understand a
seldom recognized side of addiction.

Some of the names of the characters are fictitious.

Contents

Foreword

I met Harrison Greene 52 years ago on a hilltop located on Pleiku Air Base, Vietnam, during the 1968 TET Offensive. We were both NCOs trying to do our part in the war. A few weeks later, I left Vietnam, and except for his brief visit with my wife and me in the Philippines several months later, we lost touch for some 47 years. However, Harrison is one of those special people who enter your life and never leave even though you may lose touch for long periods. Over the years, I had tried without success to locate him. Then in 2015, I found him thanks to a mutual friend on Facebook. Since then, we talk on the phone almost daily and have become the closest of friends.

Harrison lost his oldest son David to a tragic fire due to substance abuse. He was devastated, and we spoke of it for many hours until he slowly started to recover. However, the trauma associated with such a horrific event never truly leaves. Like all parents, Harrison would often ask himself if he could have done something to prevent it.

His wife, Claudia, encouraged him to face his guilt and grief. Writing the "Book of David" became his obsession for over two years.

In "The Book of David," Harrison explains how David, like many military dependents, developed the deception of resilience, the illusion that all was right with them when in reality, it was not. David was especially good at this until it started to manifest itself in addiction and irresponsible behavior. This book is about Harrison's life and how the circumstances and path of that life lent to David's "deception of resilience." What happened to David and Harrison and his entire family was primarily caused by the aftermath of military life and war. As we know so well, heartbreak and damaged lives persist long after the guns fall silent. Participants, as well as their loved ones, continue to suffer in ways they may barely realize.

Harrison bares his soul in this book, describing intimate details of his life that have been repressed for years. This story is compelling because it

1

could be told by thousands upon thousands of veterans and their family members who have suffered and are still suffering from the aftermath of war. By reading "the Book of David," they may learn they are not alone and that their suffering is not because of any wrongdoing on their part. I believe reading "The Book of David" will be an essential step in healing those emotional wounds.

Ken Sayler
Virginia Beach

Author:
Taong Labas-2014
Badger's Burrow-2020

Prologue

Judy Davis is a motivational speaker, author, and blogger who writes about military children. She observes that military kids develop a common coping skill — deception — they learn how to disguise their genuine fears to protect themselves and their families. She writes:

"Somewhere along the line, our military kids have gotten so good at protecting us that they feel the need to hide that they are suffering themselves. Resilient and strong is what they would have us believe. Still, the reality is that our military dependents need us more than ever."

David was a military dependent during the formative years of his life. He was raised by his Mother when I served with the United States Air Force in Turkey for 18 months and then for 12 months when I was sent to Vietnam.

I left the military after eight years. David attended six different school systems because I was an absentee father who traveled most of the time professionally and whose priority was career success.

David developed the skill of deception during those years. So did his mother and sister. It was how they coped with the constant moving and with my absences. They deceived themselves into believing that they were all right with my priorities. As Judy Davis writes, "They had to disguise their true fears to protect me and felt an incredible need to be strong for our family."

David's mother and sister have never expressed their true feelings to me. Their self-deception morphed into anger toward me that never left them and has marinated within them.

David's acquired ability to deceive himself and others morphed into another type of deception — the deception of resilience. He deceived himself into thinking that he could be resilient in all aspects of his life. He clung to the belief that he was resilient enough to handle alcohol and drugs.

He wasn't.

This is the story of resilience gone mad.

PART I

The Sixties

"*The sixties were about releasing ourselves from conventional society and freeing ourselves.*"

YOKO ONO

The Oak Tree

There was an oak tree in the backyard of my home when I was a boy. It was reputed to be 350 years old. Four men were barely able to wrap their arms around its trunk. I sat uninterrupted under that tree for hours. It was my most sacred place.

I told it secrets that I shared with no one.

When I remember the tree, I can smell it. I can remember how the trunk felt. I was able to grab onto the bark — it let me feel safe. It felt like the bark was grabbing onto me, too. We bonded — that oak tree and I.

I seldom tried to climb it. The first branches were too high for me to reach, and it was too massive to shinny. I once asked my Dad to lift me to the first branch and sat up there for a few minutes. But, as I sat on that branch, I felt like I was violating the sanctity of the relationship the tree and I had formed. The connection I had with the oak tree allowed me to understand integrity, honesty, respect, self-esteem, words' power, and the challenge to always be impeccable with them.

In the years to come, I would face my life's greatest challenge — imbuing David with these values that would stretch my psyche in ways I never imagined. I spent fifty years attempting to raise David with these values and watched him attempt to adopt them as he matured.

Aliquippa, Pennsylvania ▪ 1961

Main Street ends at the entrance tunnel to the Jones and Laughlin Steel Corporation. At one time, 17,000 workers passed through the tunnel each day to sign in for work. (By 1968, only about 600 workers remained. America had lost its edge on manufacturing steel. The mill was demolished, and the town never recovered).

Everything in the entire Beaver Valley of Pennsylvania seemed to be dependent on the mill. It seemed like everyone in the school had a father, grandfather, or uncle who worked there.

I attended Hopewell High School, in Hopewell Township, outside the city limits of Aliquippa. I met Barbara while on a lunch break. I was the President of the Class of 1961, and Barbara was in the Class of 1962. She wandered into the lobby one Thursday and started to talk to me. I was immediately attracted to her. She was somewhat shy but had an engaging personality and an attractive figure. Everyone liked Barbara. Her brown eyes and shapely figure caught my eye, and she seemed to like me. Our lunchtime conversations in the lobby and our physical attraction resulted in asking her for a date. Since I had my own car, Barbara insisted that I meet her mother, June. June knew my father to be an authority on health because he showed nutrition movies to students. Dad was the public relations representative for the Southerland Dairy and had received a lot of newspaper coverage in Aliquippa. Everyone recognized him because of his sculpted mustache, gorgeous business wardrobe, and ability to speak like a celebrity. June and I hit it off really well. She had respect for my Father and was glad that Barbara was dating the President of the Class of 1961. She permitted us to go out in my car with restrictions on a time limit when Barbara had to be home.

Barbara's home life was not ideal. Her father was a steelworker and had a drinking problem. He was a drunk who came home from work after stopping by the local bar for beer and shots. After an hour or so, he would arrive back from the bar, sit down at the kitchen table, always complain about the meal, and then go to the living room or bed. He would awaken at 5:00 AM the next morning, ready to go to the mill.

These binges would also be accompanied, at times, by verbal and physical abuse that stayed in the home. Months would go by like this, and suddenly, he would stop drinking and become an ideal father and husband. He was the most helpful guy you would ever want to know when he was sober. He had an outward personality and a laugh that would make others laugh also. He was always kind to me when he was sober and seemed glad that Barbara was dating me.

Barbara and I were soon 'going steady' and spent every free moment together. I had several part-time jobs. I caddied at the golf course. I had a paper route when I was 12 years old until I was 16. Then, I cleaned the windows of stores in a shopping plaza. I sold Merlite Light Bulbs door-to-door after school to homeowners in the area. These bulbs had a written guarantee stating that Merlite Light Bulb Company would send a new light bulb if their bulbs burned out. I spent $200.00 of my earnings from other jobs to purchase the bulbs. I was hugely successful and sold all of them for a total of $500.00 — a $300.00 profit. Barbara would accompany me and was amazed that I could earn so much money so quickly.

I had more cash in my pocket than most kids did because I hustled after school. I intuitively knew how to make money. I purchased a 1955 Chevy sedan, so Barbara and I could travel to Pittsburgh to take advantage of life in "the big city." My classmates wondered where I got the money for all of this. They thought my Dad was wealthy. He always wore a suit and tie. He had a handlebar mustache, a distinctive baritone voice, and an extroverted, charismatic personality. Little did my friends know that we were just getting by. I was self-supporting from the age of twelve.

Barbara and I had one passionate hobby — exploring and experimenting with our sexual energy. We became ardent devotees of the fine art of "parking" in secluded places. One of our favorites was to park in a field on a large hill that overlooked the steel mill. The mill was built along the Ohio River as it flowed north toward Ohio. The view of the blast furnaces, shooting smoke, and flames high into the night sky were breathtaking. We accompanied these impressive blasts with eruptions of our own. It was an experience no one could ever forget.

After graduation from high school, I entered college as a freshman. Barbara was in her senior year of high school. I enrolled in a small liberal arts college on the advice of my high school guidance counselor. I chose to study public speaking, drama, and communications.

Barbara and I were able to see each other occasionally during college breaks. When I finished my freshman year of college, I chose to drop out because my parents did not have enough money to help me continue. I decided to take a break and get a job to earn enough to return to college.

Barbara seemed to be another person when I returned. I called her to get together. I could sense in her voice that something had changed. She chatted for a few minutes and then said, "I am now dating someone else and think we should take a break. He has just returned from the Army, and I always wanted to be with him." My first question was, "Are you sexually involved with him." Her immediate response was, "Yes." It was over. The love affair that was Based primarily on sex was just that. But I was no longer the one she wanted. The old expression, "absence makes the heart grow fonder," took on an added twist — "for somebody else."

I was devastated, and my parents were worried about me. I could think of nothing else except my girl having sex with someone else. I did not return to college because my parents did not have the money to help me. I took a job at an Army Nike Missle Base in Coraopolis, PA, as a warehouseman, short-order cook, and janitor at the Base Exchange. I listened to the Ray Charles album I Can't Stop Loving You every evening.

My father was sympathetic to my despondency and arranged for me to attend a cocktail party at the home of his boss, William, so I could meet his daughter. They lived in Mt. Lebanon, a suburb of Pittsburgh. We arrived at their home at 7:00 PM. After greeting my mother and father, William introduced me to his wife and to Diane. Her mother reminded me of Margaret in the TV program, Father Knows Best—the epitome of proper conduct and a subtle white upper-middle-class superiority. Diane was a stunning girl who had long blond hair, blue eyes, and her own Chevy convertible. My immediate feeling was, Thank You, Dad! Diane and I were immediately attracted to each other. She suggested that we get out of the house and invited me to the Friday Night high Mt. Lebanon High School football game. She insisted that I drive her Chevy. It started to rain on the way to the game. We arrived at the stadium to find that the game had been canceled because lightning was forecast. Diane suggested that we drive around Mt. Lebanon so I could get a lay of the land. She was easy to get to know and was very open with her feelings and emotions. I enjoyed being with her and wanted to get to know her better. The rain had driven everyone indoors, and most of the stores had already closed. Diane suggested that we take a drive into the countryside.

Mt. Lebanon is surrounded by many hills and borders farm country. She directed me to turn onto a road that led up and down one hill and then up another. We were in farm country and seemed to be surrounded by cornfields. She told me to turn onto an access road leading into one of the fields. After driving on the road for approximately 100 yards, she told me to pull over on the side of the access road and told me to park the car.

Diane was an amiable girl and immediately slid closer to me and put her arms around me. I did not need an instruction manual to understand what I should do next. I pulled her closer to me and began to make love to her. Suddenly a lightning bolt struck the ground a few yards from the car. It seemed like an ocean of rain surrounded us. The thunder was deafening. Diane and I were no longer in the mood for love — we wanted to immediately get out of that field.

I started the car and put it in gear to drive. It would not budge. I tried to go forward and then quickly in reverse to rock the car. No luck. We were stuck. I tried to open the door and was shocked to find that I could only open the door an inch or so. The car had sunk into the mud up and over the doors. We knew we could not get out. The radio and power windows were dead because we had drained the battery.

"We have to get out of this car, Diane," I said. We have to get to safety."

"Let's wait until the rain tapers off," she said.

"Ok, I hope it ends quickly."

The rain slowly tapered off as the thunderstorm and rain slowly moved out of the area. Now, I had to figure out how to get out of the car. The power windows would not work. The doors were jammed by the mud.

"Diane, I am going to cut through the convertible top so we can get out of here."

"I don't care about the roof. It can be replaced. Just get us out of here."

So, I grabbed my pocket knife and cut the beautiful convertible top. When the hole became big enough, I helped Diane out and followed her. The drop to the ground was only about three feet. The car had sunk into the mud up to the wheel wells. We jumped.

We were out! We hugged each other and kissed deeply as we were laughing at the ordeal. At that moment, it seemed like a comedy. We started to walk out of the cornfield, down the access road, and finally reached the main road that led down the mountain.

We were drenched and cold. We walked about a mile. We finally reached the bottom of the hill at a crossroads. We were ecstatic when we saw a payphone booth on the side of the road. We were no longer laughing. It was 2:00 AM when Diane called her father.

Diane was sobbing when she spoke to her father. She told him what happened and where we were. He was furious and told her, "Don't move. Stay there. I will be there in twenty minutes." Diane told me, "This ride home is not going to be pretty."

Twenty minutes later, we could hear tires screeching and could see the headlights of a car speeding down the adjoining hill. We had no doubt about who was in that car. It speedily crossed the intersection. The tires squealed when it stopped. Our fathers had arrived. Her father angrily screamed at us, "Get in the car. We slid into the back seat. Her father was out of control, and he screamed at me. "You are a rapist, and you will never see my daughter again. I can only imagine what went on. You are a god damned rapist."

Diane said, "Daddy, Harrison didn't do anything to me. We were scared to death in the storm and could only…"

"Shut your mouth — he is no damn good.". You will pay for this".

My father sat in the passenger seat and did not say a word. I felt that he was not man enough to defend me. His silence was disgusting. I realized he did not want to confront William for fear of losing his job—the best paying job he ever had.

My mother and Diane's mother walked out of the house. Dad was already in the car. Diane's mother seemed to be so distant and aloof. I felt that she looked down at our family. Her father yelled, "He is a loser." Diane's mother had a disgusted look on her face and stared at me.

I tried to apologize, but Diane's father would not even look at me. My mother and I got into our car with my Dad, and he drove off. My mother asked what had happened —I told her the entire story. She believed me. I knew she was on my side. Dad did not have much to say. I think he felt humiliated. Dad did not reprimand me, and we didn't discuss it in the days to come. He knew I had acted like a gentleman with Diane.

A week passed, and I wrote Diane's father and mother a letter of apology and told them that I would be happy to pay for the convertible roof that I cut. I wrote that I was looking forward to seeing Diane again. My father went to work and reported that William had calmed down and considered my seeing Diane again.

Diane and I agreed to have another date. I arrived at her home and apologized again to her parents. They told me how much they appreciated my letter and said that I was welcome to date Diane in the future. I had dinner with the family. Diane and I went into the living room and talked about our stuck-in-the-mud experience. While her parents could not hear our conversation, they kept their eyes on us all evening. Diane said she hoped her parents would understand but regretted that she had taken me into the cornfield. Since I was spending the night there, they showed me to a bedroom on the other side of the house, far removed from Diane's. I could hear her father roaming around during the night, ensuring that I was in the assigned bedroom.

At breakfast the next morning, Diane and I talked about getting together again. I phoned her several times, but she seemed unenthusiastic.

I suspected that her parents told her that she could do better than a guy from Aliquippa. I knew that it was over — it faded away.

Ironically, William fired my Dad a few months later because he was not spending enough time in the evenings dining with his clients. William told Dad that his job was to provide the clients with whatever it took to satisfy their needs. I admire my Dad for not wanting to be a pimp for the clients.

The entire episode convinced me that the only girl I wanted in my life was Barbara. I decided to wait a few more months to see if she would call me.

She did. Six months later, on a Saturday afternoon, my mother answered the phone and told me that Barbara was on the line and asked to speak to me. I could not disguise my joy and immediately arranged a date with her. She had quit dating the army veteran because she felt he made her think that she was just another bimbo he needed to seduce. We resumed our love affair. I felt whole again. I was blinded by the light, as the rock singer Meatloaf would declare. I was in denial and acted as if nothing had happened.

I continued to work at the Army Exchange while Barbara and I planned our future. I knew that I would be financially unable to return to college. I joined the Air Force because they offered a way to get a college degree in off-duty hours. We decided that we would marry after Basic Training and Tech School.

Basic Training was at Lackland Air Force Base in San Antonio, Texas. It was an eight-month program designed to psychologically prepare recruits from all walks of life for jobs that required duty, honor, and service. We were taught that there are no prima donnas and that we would be judged only by how well we performed and adopted the Air Force's way of living. There was no my way, your way, or their way— there was only the Air Force way. I enjoyed Basic Training and learned how to integrate the Air Force's core values into lessons I learned sitting under the Oak Tree. I could now add duty and honor to those values.

During the second half of Basic Training, we were given a mandated skills assessment to determine what career field we would be assigned. My scores indicated that I had the psychological makeup and aptitude for learning Air Traffic Control. Until that moment, I had no idea what Air Traffic Controllers did except to communicate with airplanes. I did know that my profile showed that I adapted quickly to stress, and Air Traffic Control was one of the most stressful jobs in the world. I was thrilled to be selected and anxious to get started.

Eight weeks of Basic Training ended with a graduation ceremony followed by a bus ride from San Antonio to Keesler AFB in Biloxi, Mississippi. I sat with my bunk-mate, Jim Lewis, who was also selected to become an air traffic controller. We remained bunk-mates and became best friends at Keesler. Little did we know that we would be reunited on An Khe mountain in the Central Highlands of Vietnam.

Biloxi and Beyond ▪ 1963

Air Traffic Control School was a six-month training program in Biloxi that included a two-week break after three months — contingent on passing the mid-term test. I knew I had to pass that test because Barbara and I planned to be married during the two-week break. The training was from 8:00 AM to 5:00 PM. Jimmy and I were in the same class and spent our evening hours talking about our futures, how good it would be to live in our own homes. We walked through the Officer's Housing Area. Before sunset, the dusk allowed us to see families in their homes, have dinner, and watch TV. I told Jimmy that Barbara and I were looking forward to life on an Air Force Base, living in Base housing, and raising a family together. Jimmy was a fan of spy novels and said he was looking to learn more about spy agencies in the future.

I passed the first half of the Air Traffic Control School. I phoned Barbara and told her that I passed the tests and would take the first flight to Pittsburgh to marry her.

We married in a small church—I in my dress uniform and Barbara in a simple wedding dress. Barbara's parents hosted a reception in the backyard of their home for fifty relatives and friends. Many of the guests had not seen each other for years. Everyone seemed to enjoy the party. Barbara's parents were proud of their only daughter. Her father had been alcohol-free for a few weeks and was a terrific host. We could hardly wait to begin our honeymoon. I was pleased to see that our parents enjoyed each other's company. They had never spent any time together and seemed to enjoy the wedding. We mingled with all of the guests and thanked them for their gifts and for coming to our wedding. Later in the evening, we left the reception and drove to Harrisburg, PA, the state capital, for three days of bliss. We had no particular reason to honeymoon in Harrisburg except it was the state capitol and was only a four-hour drive. We checked into a hotel and visited the state capitol and historical site for two days. We had little interest in doing much except spending as much time as we could in bed — we were on our honeymoon. We returned to Aliquippa two days after arriving in Harrisburg to spend time with both of our parents. They were sad to see us leave, not knowing when we would be returning home because I had no idea where I would be assigned after graduation.

We were anxious to travel to Biloxi to complete the remainder of my Air Traffic Control Training. We packed the car full of clothes and our wedding presents, said goodbye to our parents, and drove to Biloxi, Mississippi — an 18 hour, 1000 mile trip. We arrived in Biloxi during a heavy rainstorm. The heat and humidity took our breath away.

We stopped at a pizza place to have dinner, and when we returned to our car, it had been broken into and robbed. Most of our clothes were stolen. The police who arrived sarcastically told us, "Hey, this is Biloxi, and we have gangs that beak into cars every day. Welcome to Biloxi." We just had to suck it up. We drove to the Base and checked into the transient enlisted quarters for the night

The next day we found a one-bedroom furnished flat on Reynoir Street. The rent was $ 55.00 per month. It was close to the Base and served as our temporary home until I finished the second half of my training before a permanent assignment to parts unknown after graduation.

We enjoyed our life in Biloxi. I would finish training each day at 4:00 PM. We had every evening and weekend to ourselves. We spent most of our time exploring the town. Biloxi was racially segregated, but the rebellious liberal streak in us compelled us to disregard all of the 'whites-only' signs we encounterd. We sat in the 'colored only' section of the soda fountain at the drug store. We used the 'colored only' water fountains and restrooms. No one confronted our behavior. They just seemed to look the other way. They could see that I was military, I think, by my haircut and a northern accent. We were unafraid.

The heat and humidity in August were as thick as cooking fat. You could not only feel it — you could also smell it. Our tiny apartment was not air-conditioned. The bedroom was like a sauna, and we relied on a floor fan to keep us fresh during the steamy, sweaty nights of sex that we found so irresistible as newlyweds. It was during one of those sultry nights in August 1963 that David was conceived. He was now a vital part of our life.

The First Tarmac ▪ 1963

Graduation from the Air Traffic Control School was not joyful — it was heartbreaking because the graduation certificate was accompanied by orders to my first duty station. I was assigned to an unaccompanied 18-month tour of duty at Incirlik Air Base, Turkey. It was the unaccompanied part that rocked our world. I did not have sufficient rank to bring Barbara with me at Air Force expense. I would have to leave her and our first yet unborn child behind.

I received a 30-day leave before departing for Turkey. We drove north to visit our parents in Aliquippa. We took my best friend and bunkmate, Jimmy, with us. He was African American and was hesitant to ride with us through Mississippi, Alabama, and the Carolinas. He was a black guy riding in a car with a white man and a white woman — not a welcome sight in the segregated south in the 1960s. Jimmy lay on the floor in the car's back seat each time we stopped. We brought food out to him. We stopped at secluded rest stops to use the facilities. We were fearful of reprisal should he be discovered in the car with us. We felt very relieved when we passed through Virginia and the other states north of the Mason-Dixon line.

After a 16 hour drive, we arrived at his hometown, Keyser, West Virginia. We hugged him and said goodbye. We had no idea if we would ever meet again.

It took us three hours to drive from Keyser to Aliquippa. We visited our parents during my 30-day leave. I tried to secure help from my local congressman in hopes that he could get me reassigned. No help was forthcoming. The 18-month separation could not be appealed. We kept ourselves busy by visiting friends and relatives, shopping for maternity outfits for Barbara and baby supplies, and clothes. We alternately stayed with Barbara's parents and my parents during this leave. We watched the days pass in sorrow until the day of my departure. Saying goodbye to our parents was a gut-wrenching experience.

Barbara drove me to the Pittsburgh airport. As we kissed each other goodbye on the tarmac with tears rolling down our cheeks, I put my head on her belly to listen to the heartbeat of our child.

I boarded a Pan Am flight to the newly opened John F. Kennedy International Airport (previously known as Idlewild Airport). The first stop was in Paris, and then to Frankfort, Rome, Athens, and finally to the Istanbul Ataturk Airport. It was there that I was introduced to squat toilets. I had no doubt that I was in an under-developed country.

I transferred to a Turkish Airlines flight to the Adana Sakripasa Airport. My soon to be Supervisor, Master Sergeant Herb Morrow, greeted me at the airport and drove me to Incirlik Air Base, a joint USAF-Turkish Air Force Base.

I arrived at Incirlik with $8.00 in my pocket and used it for meals at the dining hall until my food ration allowance showed up in my first paycheck. I walked into the Airman's Club and saw a slot machine. I deposited one quarter, pulled the handle, and won $5.00. Now I would make it until payday. I had made an allotment to Barbara to receive all of my $85.80 monthly salary and $55.20 housing allowance. I lived on my rations and overseas pay.

Since Barbara could not accompany me, she remained in our hometown. I could not afford the airfare to bring her to Turkey. If she had been able to join me would have to live in downtown Adana, Turkey, not on-Base. Rank has its privileges. We learned that Adana had the highest rate of childhood tuberculosis in the world at that time. She was two months pregnant when I left for Turkey, so not having her join me was a blessing in disguise.

Life Apart ▪ 1963-1965

An 18-month separation is especially unbearable for wives left behind. Barbara lived by herself in a small apartment in our hometown, equidistance between her parents and mine. She handled our separation alright for the first few months and responded to my daily letters as often as she could. Soon the newness of living alone in her apartment, coupled with the excitement of giving birth, wore off. Letters from her became far and few between. Barbara was too depressed and could not communicate with me. A telephone call from her was not possible. A phone call from me required taking a bus to the telephone company in Adana, waiting in line for at least two hours, and then call her. The going rate then was $32.00 a minute, an expense I could not afford.

Barbara was two months pregnant when I left. She knew that half of my 18-month tour would be over when our child was born. Barbara would have to raise the baby by herself for eleven months while she waited for me. Her small one-bedroom flat was close to both our parents. She was able to count on their help when needed.

I was distraught with worry because Barbara was not keeping me informed about her life and pregnancy. My supervisor's wife, Joanne, consoled me and tried to keep me focused on the bright side. At one point, I had to ask the Red Cross to check on Barbara's well-being — they verified that she was OK. I could not take leave to be with her for our baby's birth because I could not pay for a plane flight. We waited in silence.

Life for me at Incirlik Air Base was consumed by learning the intricacies of becoming a rated air traffic controller. It was all-consuming, but I obtained ratings in both the control tower and radar approach control facility in short order. Controllers lived, slept, and ate air traffic control 24 hours a day. When not on duty, we were at the Airman's club or the dining hall or snack-bar exchanging air traffic control stories.

MSgt. Herb Morrow would invite other controllers and me to his home in Base housing. I became very connected with his wife, Joanne, and three children, Pam, Doug, and Diane. They became home away from home and helped me through the loneliness I felt.

Herb had been on many tours in his career and had left his family behind many times. They knew first-hand the heartache I was experiencing. Without them, my life at Incirlik Air Base would have been almost intolerable. They made me feel like I was part of their family and knew I deeply missed Barbara and longed to be with her. Joanne was like the big sister I never had. She helped me understand what Barbara was going through.

I was assigned to the Radar Approach Control unit. Herb was the shift supervisor and helped me become proficient. One evening in the middle of the night, I controlled an F-101 fighter jet, call sign Sandy 12, returning to the Base. I assumed control of the aircraft when the pilot reported his position and requested a radar-controlled approach to Incirlik. He was at 30,000 feet and was directly over the 12,322 ft. Taurus mountains. I instructed him to descend and maintain 4500 feet and to report when he was level at 4500 ft. He responded with "Roger, descend and maintain 4,500". A few seconds passed, and I looked at my radar scope and realized I had told him to descend directly over the mountain. Sweat broke out on my face and neck, and I could hear my pulse in my ears. I quickly transmitted, "Sandy 12, climb immediately and maintain 20,000 ft. Report level at 20,000." He knew that unless he was having an emergency, he was required to climb immediately. The pilot responded, "Roger, climb and maintain 20,000." A few seconds passed. As I looked at my radar screen, I realized I had descended the pilot into a valley between two sides of the mountain. My heart raced. The next thing I heard was, "Approach Control, Sandy 12, level, 20000." The pilot was out of danger. I was so grateful I almost fainted.

Herb sensed that I was not myself and asked me what was happening. I told him. He told me to take a break outside the radar unit and that he would assume control of Sandy 12. He knew I was a mental wreck. After he had Sandy 12 under control, executing a safe approach to the Base, he told the pilot to contact the Control Tower for landing instructions. He walked outside of the unit and said, "I know you will never make that mistake again, Airman. Now, get back in there and control some more aircraft the way you know how!"

I devoted myself to my job because I wanted to be an excellent controller. I loved the excitement and adrenaline rush all controllers receive working under pressure. I had a 48-hour break between shifts and mostly hung around the Base and often visited Herb's family since he and I were both off duty at the same time each shift. They became my home away from home, and I never abused their generosity. They taught me the value of true friendship.

I took only one three-day pass during the 18 months at Incirlik. Winston McCarty, a fellow controller and friend, and I took a micro-mini bus to Ankara, Turkey's capital. Men, women, and their children filled the van. Some of them even brought their goats and chickens. Many rode on the roof, and others hung out of the windows.

A fascinating part of the trip was the drive through the formidable Taurus Mountains. The mini-bus driver would stop every three hours. Everyone would walk into a nearby field and relieve themselves en masse. No one minded the cramped seats and odorous scents of humans and their animals co-mingling. Mini-buses were the way you traveled in Turkey when you had no money for airfare. We could only hope that our trip would be safe.

The Taurus mountains were magnificent, and at times the road was very treacherous. Finally, after an all-day trip, we arrived in Ankara. The two days we spent in Ankara were spent primarily at the NCO Club. We ate there and enjoyed the Manhattans and Old Fashioneds at the bar, served in punch bowls. We couldn't stop imbibing. I don't remember leaving the club and returning to the enlisted airman visitor quarters. Somehow we were able to find our way and awakened the next morning with hangovers. We toured Ankara near the club but did not have enough money to see all of the city.

We grabbed another mini-bus for our return trip to Incirlik the next day. Our short stay in Ankara provided a welcome respite from life on the

Base. The three-day pass I had was the only real-time off during the 18 months I was in Incirlik except for scheduled breaks between shifts.

On one of those breaks, another friend, Tony, and I took a mini-bus trip to Iskenderun, a port city on the Mediterranean. We enjoyed wine with fresh tomatoes and cucumbers with loaves of fresh bread while overlooking the Mediterranean's beautiful blue waters. We drank too much and were both in no condition to return to Incirlik. Fortunately, the proprietor of the restaurant insisted that we remain in the restaurant. He gave us head and shoulder massages and a decanter of water with lemons until he felt we were sober enough to get on the bus to return to the Base. The beauty of the day and the caring friendship of the Turkish proprietor never left my memory. Iskenderun reminded me of National Geographic Magazine photographs. Simple. Beautiful.

Other than these adventures, I remained on-Base. I spent two Thanksgivings and two Christmases at Incirlik during those 18 months. Herb and Joanne welcomed the unaccompanied controllers to enjoy Thanksgiving and Christmas at their home on Base. Our cups flowed over with love and friendship and appreciation for Joanne and Herb's hospitality.

The days and weeks and months soon became very routine, and time seemed to drag. I eagerly went to the mailroom every day in hopes that I would receive a letter from Barbara. Very few ever arrived. Barbara seemed to have removed me from her mind. I was sick at heart.

I eagerly awaited news of the birth of our child. One evening when Winston and I were taking a walk around the Base, an airman who worked in the communications center told me to report to the office. I had a tele-gram from the Red Cross. It informed me that I was now the father of a healthy son. Winston and I were jubilant. Barbara and I had decided that if the baby was a boy, we would name him David. Winston and I celebrated David's birth at the Airman's Club. (Winston noted David's birth date and called David or me on his birthday every year afterward.)

I anxiously awaited further word about his birth and how Barbara was doing. I finally received a letter from my mother, telling me that Barbara had a relatively easy delivery. She wrote that both of them were doing well and that David was a bright, healthy boy. I hoped to hear from Barbara, but it was a few weeks until I received a letter from her. Her letters were infrequent, and she sent no pictures. My parents had no explanation and said they thought she was doing fine, but they did not elaborate. At one point, I had to contact the Red Cross to get more information. They assured me that she was too depressed to write to me.

I completed all of my required on-the-job training while working for Master Sergeant Morrow and was promoted to Airman Second Class. He was the most exceptional Air Traffic Control supervisor and mentor I had during my service. Everyone knew Herb cared about them and their success.

Finally, my 18-month tour of duty in Turkey came to an end. I joyfully flew from Adana, Turkey to London, and then to New York's JFK International Airport, newly renamed from Idlewild in 1963. I dressed in civilian clothes to feel like a civilian. I wore a Harris Tweed sport coat and a new pair of trousers that I purchased from a men's tailor shop at Incirlik Air Base. I felt cosmopolitan for the first time in eighteen months.

As I walked through the terminal at JFK, I was struck by the cultural changes that had occurred in the United States in just 18 months. It seemed as if a revolution in clothing had arrived while I was gone; the United States seemed like another world to me after living in Adana, Turkey. American women had to wear very modest attire on Base to not offend Islamic tradition. They seldom ventured into Adana. . I was amazed and excited to see young women in mini-skirts and knee-high boots.

I called Barbara from a payphone immediately after landing at JFK. As soon as I heard her voice, I broke into tears. I was without words and could only tell her when my flight would land at the Greater Pittsburgh Airport, where she, David, and my parents would meet me. The flight from New York to Pittsburgh seemed longer than the flight to New York from Turkey.

David and I were united as I stepped off the airplane at the Pittsburgh airport when I returned. As I jubilantly walked down the steps onto the tarmac (there were no jetways in 1965), Barbara and my parents were standing there eagerly waiting for me. Their happiness to see me was energizing. I was home. David was in his Mother's arms. He immediately recognized me because Barbara put pictures of me in his crib and told him stories about me. She put him on the tarmac, and he ran to me. My blonde-haired, brown-eyed son jumped into my arms.

It was a moment neither of us would forget. As Barbara embraced me, a new chapter had begun in our lives. I was now Daddy in the flesh. Our bonding had started on an airport tarmac. Our love had endured, and our family had a new beginning. A new challenge was about to begin.

A Semblance of Normalcy ▪ 1965

A massive cultural change had taken place in the United States while I was gone. A musical phenomenon called the Beetles emerged on the rock and roll scene. Rock and Roll was the music of the day. There were new stores like K-Mart and McDonalds that seemed to be invading every town. Almost everyone had color television, and people seemed to be glued to it every evening. There were new television programs I had never watched. The Lucy Show, The Dean Martin Show, and The Beverly Hillbillies were on everyone's must-watch list.

I was enthralled with David. He and I bonded very quickly. I wanted to do everything for him, from changing his diaper to feeding him. Naturally, Barbara was a bit uncomfortable with my jumping right in and seemed a little jealous that I was now consuming a lot of David's time. But, she quickly accepted my enthusiasm and knew that David was in good hands with his Dad. She wanted to teach me everything I didn't know about the right and wrong way to care for him, and I was an eager learner.

We visited with our parents during the 30-day leave. I was excited to think that they would have many questions about what life was like in Turkey. I asked them many questions about David's birth and his activities during the ten months after he was born before I returned. But it seemed that they were satisfied just to know I had returned.

I brought presents back from Turkey for my parents and Barbara's — a genuine Meerschaum pipe for Barbara's father. I gave her mother a beautiful silk headscarf, and I gave a traditional Turkish silk shawl to my mother. My Dad loved the hand-carved bookends I gave him. It was fun being with them and made me realize how important they were to me. They were glad to know that we would be living at Wurtsmith AFB in Oscoda, Michigan, an eight-hour drive from Aliquippa. Barbara. David and I alternately stayed with her parents and mine during those thirty days. We went shopping for clothes for David and Barbara. We visited with everyone for two weeks and then said, see you later, as we bid them goodbye. We were excited to get on the road to Oscoda, Michigan, to begin a new life at Wurtsmith Air Force Base.

Oscoda was a sleepy little town on the eastern shore of Lake Michigan. It was "above the thumb of Michigan, on Route 23", as the residents would say. Oscoda was a frequent stop for travelers, but the town derived most of its revenue from Wurtsmith Air Force Base. Naturally, a few industries were primarily devoted to Michigan's abundant supply of lumber and to selling outdoor gear for camping, canoes, and travel equipment. Lumberman's Monument was a popular tourist attraction. A few bars and restaurants attracted the Base guys, but there was very little for families to do. (When the Department of Defense closed Wurtsmith in 1993, the population of the town dropped from 3000 (mostly Air Force families) to fewer than 1000 permanent residents.

Since I did not have enough rank to live in Base housing, we found our first little home on Lake Huron's bank in downtown Oscoda, Michigan. It was a very small two-bedroom cottage that we rented for $85.00 a month and turned into a comfortable home for the three of us. It was one of the happiest times of our marriage.

During those three years at Wurtsmith Air Base, we enjoyed life to the extent that an airman's meager monthly salary could afford. At one point, I had to redeem the silver dollars that I had saved since a child to buy milk for David and needed groceries for us. Many airmen had to work part-time jobs to supplement their income to avoid food stamps. I worked part-time as a janitor in a local laundromat. Barbara also found a job there as an attendant during the days. We now had a bit of discretionary income.

Air Traffic Controllers worked one day from 8:00 AM until 4:00 PM, followed by working from 4:00 PM until Midnight the next day, and then from Midnight to 8:00 AM the third day. Then there was a 48-hour break, and the cycle resumed. It was not an ideal schedule to allow quality time with Barbara and David. He was always ready to play and explore with me after I finished the Midnight to 8:00AM shift in the control tower. Barbara was lonesome during those shifts. But it sure was better than being exiled from them in Turkey for 18 months.

In our free time, we ensured that we did things as a family in the local area. We had very little disposable income. We drove a fuel-efficient Opal that enabled us to explore the destinations in and around Oscoda and the beaches of Lake Huron. A drive to the 'big city.' Bay City, 90 miles south, was an occasional destination to shop at Sears. But, our life centered on David. He was a one-year-old, vibrant little boy, full of energy and enthusiasm. We took him with us wherever we went. He was fun to be with because of the variety of questions popped from his brain like popcorn pops in a kettle.

A significant entertainment source for David was sitting in our car in front of the local appliance store. It had a huge glass window. We parked in front of the window in the parking lot to watch color television. We enjoyed it even though we could not hear it, and provided us a way to get out of our little cottage for an hour or so — the small pleasures of a simple life.

One of the biggest thrills we had was winning a brand new color TV in a drawing of tickets from the Wurtsmith AFB Credit Union annual meeting. We were intrigued by it because we were able to view TV in living color. It became very inexpensive entertainment for us and meant we would not have to sit in front of the appliance store. David was fascinated with the color television and seldom missed an episode of Mister Roger's Neighborhood or Davey and Goliath.

Our cottage was just two blocks from Lake Huron. David loved to go to the beach and play in the surf and sand. We spent many hours walking along that beach, answering David's never-ending questions about the crabs, the fish, the waves, and the tide. He loved to be buried in the sand so that only his head remained visible. We shared a million laughs. He was a joy for us. Our family had bonded again, and we relished it.

I advanced quickly as an air traffic controller and was fortunate to be promoted to the rank of Airman First Class and then to Staff Sergeant. We agreed that I should re-enlist for a second four-year term, and I did on February 19,1967.

We were now qualified to live on the Base in enlisted housing. I was given a $5000.00 reenlistment bonus. Eagerly, we moved into a three-bedroom single-family home on Base. It was a dream home for us, and we quickly furnished it using most of the bonus money. Life was coming together nicely for us. David had his own bedroom and lots of playmates from the neighborhood. We socialized more with the friends we made. I was now earning enough to enable us to have a better life. We relished in it.

It was the best of times for David.

The worst of times came in 1968 on another tarmac.

The Second Tarmac ▪ 1968

On a cloudy and chilly day in January 1968, four-year-old David came face-to-face with the Vietnam War's reality at the regional airport serving Midland, Bay City, and Saginaw, Michigan. At his age, he didn't understand it but certainly was traumatized by it.

We never expected that I would be sent to Vietnam after I re-enlisted in 1967. I had just returned in 1965 from an unaccompanied eighteen-month tour of duty in Turkey. I was mistaken. Barbara and I both felt like we were going to be in exile again. We both knew how painful the 18-month separation had been for both of us. We were afraid of what another twelve more months would do to our marriage.

I appealed this assignment through Air Force channels. It seemed to be a cruel and unusual punishment to separate again a family who had just endured an 18-month separation fewer than two years previously. My appeal fell on deaf ears. Air Force needed air traffic controllers in Vietnam and were classified as "mission-critical".

David was too young to understand the full impact of this on his life. He was ill-prepared to lose his father for a year. What can you say to a little four-year-old boy who is about to have his father abandon him for 365 days? We had just learned how to love each other.

The day of my departure came much too quickly. So, here we were at yet another tarmac. My parents came to visit us at Wurstmith AFB before my departure on this year-long assignment in Vietnam. We lived on an Air Force Base, but we had to drive 111 miles to the Midland-Saginaw-Bay City airport so that I could catch a flight to Travis AFB in San Francisco. Barbara and David would remain on the Base in Base housing until I returned.

Boarding time came too quickly. The airplane pulled up next to the terminal. I was the only military person to board the airplane. We waited until the very last minute and exchanged hugs and kisses — our eyes filled with tears. Barbara was acting strong for David. I picked him up and held him tightly and told him that I loved him with all my heart and would return to be with him forever. I told him his mother loved him and would take good care of him. She was beside herself with grief.

I hugged my mother and father. They were heartbroken and terrified, also. I was their only son, and I was leaving for a war zone. We kissed and said goodbye. We did not know if we would ever again say hello in person. There were no words.

David's Grandpa walked to him and picked him up to hold him in his arms. They both were sobbing. It was all my Dad could do to restrain David from running to me. Tears ran down my Dad's face, and he was shaking while he held David. Barbara and my Mother were in shock and were crying uncontrollably. An unspoken question permeated everyone's mind— would I return alive and uninjured?

I grabbed David into my arms and held on to Barbara as if holding them would make it impossible for me to walk to that airplane. A goodbye kiss seemed meaningless. I looked into Barbara's eyes. The tears were running down her cheeks, but her eyes were devoid of feeling. She was numb with fear. I hugged her with all my strength. I was abandoning her and David again. That feeling was devastatingly powerful. I have never forgotten it.

I put David down and started to walk across the tarmac to the boarding steps after all of the passengers were on board the aircraft —David would have none of this. He ran to me and grabbed my pants leg while he cried out, "Please don't go, Daddy... don't go!" That plea I once spoke to my father echoed in my head. David's grandfather took him into his arms. I climbed the stairs to the door of the airplane. The flight attendant looked at me with tears in her eyes. I looked back. They were frozen in place. I was leaving the most precious people in my life, those I loved more deeply than I could ever communicate. I turned and boarded the airplane. The one-year countdown clock was activated.

The flight attendant's announcement to buckle my seat belt came too quickly. I had left my only son, my wife, and my parents for a year. Barbara was frightened and afraid. Everyone was afraid I would die in Vietnam.

David felt abandoned. I knew it because I saw it in his eyes despite his tears. I don't think his tears ever permanently left his soul. This was simply not fair. And, in some intuitive way, I knew that I would return in twelve months — intact.

Mission Critical

Travis AFB in San Francisco was the main departure point for Air Force personnel enroute to Vietnam. I did not travel to Vietnam as part of a unit. I was one Airman boarding a TWA 707 jet loaded with civilian contractors, State Department personnel, AID personnel, and others headed to Vietnam.

I sat next to an executive from a milk company who was setting up a powdered milk plant in Saigon so the troops could have a semblance of fresh milk each day. (It wasn't bad, and I found it almost indistinguishable from real milk.) This man did not appear upset about going to Vietnam; he would only be there for a few months before returning to his family. He was not a Vietnam 'lifer'.

After refueling stops in Hawaii, Okinawa, and Guam to pick up other passengers, we arrived in Saigon to a welcoming committee of mortars and rockets. As we arrived, the pilot announced, "We have landed in Saigon. I apologize for bringing you here, and I hope I can bring you home someday."

I was at Tan Son Nuht Air Base in Saigon — but not for long. As I looked out of the terminal windows, I saw body bags being loaded into the airplane. I knew this was not going to be fun.

We quickly disembarked from the front of the 707 while others were getting on board in the rear. The pilot kept the engines running. He taxied for takeoff as soon as the cabin door was closed and made a rapid ascent out of Vietnam.

I made a rapid ascent to the nearest transient barracks to find a bunk. I found an empty bed, quickly flopped into it, and promptly fell asleep when the rockets and mortars ceased for a few moments. I was emotionally and physically exhausted. The air was heavy with the scent of mildew, sweat, human waste, and garbage. Saigon was oppressive — you could feel it. My guts ached for my family.

The next morning, I was back at the terminal, trying to find an Air Force flight to my assigned unit, Nha Trang Air Base. There were many flights to Nha Trang. I hopped on one and arrived a short time later. Upon reporting to the first sergeant, I was asked, "What the hell are you doing here, sergeant?" I showed him my orders. He said, "We don't need any other Controllers. Go somewhere else." When I asked where, he said, "Get your ass out to the flight line and fly to some other Base."

So I did. I did this three or four times, only to receive the same greeting and order. Finally, I arrived at Phu Cat Air Base, where I was told they needed Controllers to work in the Control Tower. After being there for two weeks, the First Sergeant called me into his office and told me, "I am sorry to tell you this Greene, but you have been reassigned to Pleiku." I said, "Why are you sorry," and he quietly said, "Pleiku is the most shelled Base in Vietnam. Good luck."

I arrived at Pleiku on a C-130 cargo aircraft during a heavy mortar and rocket attack. The greeting I heard was, "Welcome to Pleiku, the Pearl of Southeast Asia."

After reporting in at the 1878 Communications Squadron, I was assigned a barracks on the Main Base. The barracks was one of several two-story buildings that housed about 80 airmen who slept on double bunks with mattresses. It boggled my mind to understand why the civil engineers built a two-story barracks in an active rocket attack area. The latrines were in separate buildings and had decent showers, urinals, private sit-down stalls, and an odor of waste that never left. Vietnamese housemaids worked on the Base every morning in their Noni-la, conical-pointed straw hats. They cleaned our barracks and latrine, polished our boots, and did our laundry for $3.00 a month.

I often worried about my safety in the barracks. Housemaids might slit our throats while we slept because the Vietcong would harm or kill their children if they refused. I slept on edge during the day when housemaids were on duty. Fortunately, these women were very kind and arduous in their work. I was considerate to them and had fun engaging them in conversation. I taped some songs they sang, and they felt like celebrities. She told me I was "Numbah one."

The latrine was not a place to linger because the barracks were frequent targets of Vietcong rockets and mortars. Fortunately, my barracks never took a direct rocket or mortar hit. We routinely repaired and enlarged our sand-bagged bunkers. They provided safety during the never-ending nighttime rocket and mortar attacks. Since I was the ranking airman in the barracks, I would always be the last one out during an attack. For some odd reason, I would not leave until I had dressed entirely, combed my hair, and stood at the door as the guys ran out. I would open the door for them running in their skivvies and trip them to make sure they were crouched down when they ran toward the bunker because the shrapnel would miss them.

I was assigned to a newly installed radar facility atop a hill on the Base. It was code-named 'Peacock,' an operational radar air traffic control and training facility. Our mission was to train the South Vietnamese Controllers to control enroute U. S. Air Force and Army aircraft within our airspace. One of our essential functions was to provide artillery warnings to aircraft so they not be hit by our artillery.

The Vietnamese spoke Vietnamese, and we spoke English. The training was non-existent. The South Vietnamese controllers looked at their radar scopes. They listened to our instructions to the enroute aircraft we controlled. They occasionally issued artillery advisories to their South Vietnamese aircraft.

The most rewarding part of working at Peacock was to guide our aircraft to their destinations while they were enroute. This entailed vectoring them around other traffic and getting them to their destination safely. On any given day, the air traffic was substantial with fighter jets, cargo aircraft, helicopters, and Air Evacuation aircraft enroute to Base hospitals.

Two weeks after I arrived at Pleiku, on January 30, 1968, the Tet Offensive began. We prepared to be overrun by the North Vietnamese and Viet Cong. I was assigned with a hundred other Airmen to man the perimeter of the flight line. I jumped into a fortified foxhole with another 'Peacock' controller. Suddenly the Base was hit by a massive rocket and mortar attack. We were terrified that the enemy would break through the concertina wire 30 feet from our foxholes. Rockets and mortars fell close to us. The Vietcong launched them from outside our perimeter toward the flight line and the Base. It was night, and we could not see if the Viet Cong were advancing toward our concertina wire. We opened fire to pre-emptily stop the Viet Cong and NVA from over-running the Base. But 'Spooky,' our C-47 aircraft armed with M-61 Vulcan rotating barrel cannons, each firing 2000-6000 rounds a minute, stopped the ground invasion. Every fifth shell was a red tracer that looked like three red spaghetti strings extending from the aircraft to the ground. After the sun rose, we saw the fields outside the perimeter, littered with dead NVA and VC bodies that had been executed by the C-47's mini-guns. They all had died from head and shoulder rounds. We lost no one

Since we had a surplus of air traffic controllers, our duty hours were so short that I had a lot of free time on my hands. I decided to volunteer to be the Squadron Information NCO, to write hometown news releases about airmen in the Squadron. These human interest stories were sent to an Airman's hometown newspaper to provide family and friends with information about the Airman and provide excellent public relations to the Air Force. I also wrote stories that the Seventh Air Force in Saigon would publish in Air Force publications and stateside media.

Two months or so after I arrived at Pleiku, we received a new squadron commander, Major Edmound Orr. He was on the Base for only a few weeks when he attended The Base Commanders' monthly meeting with all squadrons' commanders.

The Base Commander presented him with the Prime Bull Award. This trophy had a water buffalo at its centerpiece and was awarded to the Squadron with the best Information Program. Major Orr knew nothing about this award and was very honored to receive it. He just didn't know why this happened.

After checking, he learned that I was responsible for the news releases and asked First Sergeant Smith to invite me to meet with him. The Major thanked me for the work I did to get the Squadron recognized. I thanked him and asked, "Major Orr, how would you like to leave here as a Lieutenant Colonel." He said, "What are you talking about, Sergeant Greene." I said, "Well, I can make that happen if you grant me three things."

"What do you need, Sergeant?"

"'I need a typewriter of my own, a little office for privacy that has a key for security. Travel orders that permit me to visit other Bases would be essential. I want to make you and the Squadron famous." He replied, "First Sergeant, give Greene whatever he needs."

I immediately flew to Saigon to meet with correspondents from the Associated Press and other journalists. I wrote stories about our Squadron's success in re-orienting air traffic control radar so that it was able to detect incoming mortars and rockets. We then could direct fighter aircraft to their location to take them out.

I needed a broader perspective about the war. In my free time, I accompanied Special Forces troops to a Montagnard village. The Montagnard people were brave and despised the Viet Cong and North Vietnam Army. They were loyal American allies. We affectionately nicknamed them "Yards."

During our visit to the village, I attended a welcoming meeting of the Montagnard chief and his leaders. They hosted a peaceful ceremony in a large, bamboo covered hut that served as their meeting place. The hut had a huge fire burning cauldron in the center. We sat in a circle while the Montagnard-speaking Special Forces translators interpreted. We all smoked from a pipe they shared with us —I have no idea what was burning in the pipe — we drank with a ladle filled with some sort of wine and cooked insects and rats. We would have insulted them if we did not drink with them—they would have been offended.

After the hut ceremony, our hosts showed us several holes that were dug in the ground. These holes were a little wider than our shoulders and were about six feet deep. These holes were covered with camouflaged lids covered with dirt, stones, and grass, much like drain covers in the streets back home. We were told if Montagnard scouts spotted VC or NVA troops, the Montagnards would lower us into the hole and put the lid on it. This gave new meaning to "put the lid on this." We would stay there until the VC or NVA departed the village. No one knew how long they would remain in the village. The VC and NVA feared the Montagnards because they would outfight them and were more violent than the VC.

I was terrified and could not wait to leave and return to the Base. Our stay lasted for only an hour or so. The helicopter that picked us up was the most beautiful aircraft I had ever seen. Wop, wop, wop — we were gone.

The Montagnards were instrumental in providing intelligence about enemy troop movement in the jungle. Our intelligence gathering was dependent on these native people. Their contribution to saving hundreds of soldier's lives has not received the respect that it deserves. Their sacrifice has never been memorialized but has never been forgotten.

The unlimited travel orders Major Orr issued enabled me to attend Information Office Conferences at Baggio in the Philippines and in Bangkok. These conferences allowed the attendees to share notes and gather ideas for additional stories.

While in the Philippines, I visited another air traffic controller stationed with me at Pleiku on temporary duty for 60 days. Ken Sayler and his Filipina wife, Leng, became life long, trusted friends. It was a thrill to spend a day with them. Ken and I reminisced about our days together at Pleiku. Leng was a wonderful host and made me feel like I was home again. They had endured unimaginable barriers to getting married in the Philippines. The military did not want GI's to marry Filipinas because of fear that if she became pregnant, the GI would simply abandon them and return to the States. Fortunately, Ken and Leng prevailed and were permitted to marry because it was evident that Ken was an honorable man and that Leng was deeply in love with Ken. Our reunion was too short, and I caught a flight back to Nam the next day. Ken and I lost contact for 47 years after our mini-reunion at Clark Air Base before meeting again. We finally met again in 2015 when a mutual friend told Ken that I was on Facebook. Ken wrote a fictional book called Taong Labas. It is about the experience of the Filipinos during the Second World War. Taong Labas became recommended reading by Filipino school children in the Philippines because of their absence of historical knowledge about that war. Ken released his second fictional book, Badger's Burrow, about the effect the Vietnam War has had on POW and their families. We eventually met each other again in 2015 but that' a story for another time

I received a phone call while I was working at Peacock. Jimmy Lewis, my bunkmate at Basic Training and at Keesler AFB, was in Vietnam at An Khe Mountain and had located me somehow. I was excited to hear from him. He invited me to join him for a couple of days at An Khe. I took a chopper from Pleiku to An Khe the following week. He greeted me at the mountain Base as I disembarked the chopper and drove me in a jeep to his duty station atop the mountain.

I lost contact with Jim after we competed Air Traffic Control School. He ended up in Japan and became involved with black market liquor stolen from the Officer's Club. The Air Force threw the book at him and ordered him to return to the U.S. for sentencing. His flight had a refueling stop in Hawaii. As he exited the airplane to go inside the terminal, he was greeted by three CIA agents who made him an offer he could not refuse. He could join them in Vietnam or return to the states to be sentenced to Leavenworth Penitentiary — a no brainer decision.

Jimmy explained that the CIA had identified him as a stoic and trained him to assassinate. He was working undercover at An Khe as an air traffic controller received assignments from time to time to execute the U.S.enemies in the Far East. The CIA would take him to a designated location where the target was living. Jimmy's job was to assassinate the person at a specific time when the CIA knew the target would be. Jimmy shared one hit he completed in Bangkok when the target was sitting on a park bench, reading the paper as he did every day. Jimmy walked along the sidewalk and shot the target in the head. He would then get on an aircraft back to An Khe, where he would resume duty.

Jimmy and I sat outside his quarters on the mountain one evening to talk about his job, my job at Peacock, and Barbara. As we talked that evening, the mountain was obscured by fog. We were drinking fine bourbon and smoking weed. All that we could see was boulders sticking up over the fog, and all we could hear was artillery passing over our heads. The Army was firing artillery over the mountain to impact the NVA in the jungle. The NVA was sending artillery rounds over the mountain to hit the Army Base. It was surreal.

Jimmy drove me to the Army Chopper Base the next day because I had to return to Pleiku. As we hugged and said goodby, Jimmy reached into his pocket and handed me $10,000. He said this was the wedding present plus interest because he could not afford to give us a wedding present after graduation from air traffic control school. I was overcome with emotion and thanked him for his kindness but told him I could not accept the money because I would have no legal way to take it out of the country. He said if I ever needed money to let him know. I returned to Pleiku and served out the rest of my tour working at Peacock and continued to write stories about our squadron. I promised to make Major Orr famous. He left Pleiku as a Lieutenant Colonel.

That was the last time I ever heard from Jimmy until a few years later when I was living at Wurtsmith AFB. I answered the phone one afternoon. Jimmy called to tell me that would be the last time I would hear from him. I asked him where he was going, and he said on assignment. I never heard from him again.

The Agony of Separation ▪ 1968

While I was dealing with Vietnam's rigors, Barbara was dealing with a nightmare of her own. It was Wurtsmith AFB. She would have access to the Base facilities. She would not have to move when I left for Vietnam or when I returned because Vets returning from Vietnam had the first choice of where they wanted to be stationed when they returned. We knew the Base would offer security and could remain close to some of the friends we had made.

Unknown to me, voyeurs harassed Barbara. She was terrified. On more than one occasion, she had to call the Base police to report them looking in the windows of our home. The air police were prompt and put the house under surveillance for a few weeks. The voyeurs never returned. But Barbara was traumatized, and she did not inform me. I assume that she did not want me to worry.

Rather than becoming involved with a limited number of activities available for a wife and child living alone on the Base, Barbara only stayed close to friends we had previously. They were supportive of her but had their own lives to lead. She knew she would be alone for the next year and became unable to cope with it. Once again, she chose to leave me out of their daily life. No letters were forthcoming on any regular basis. I sent her cassette tapes that I narrated, but she sent a few to me in return. The only information I had about her or David was what my parents relayed to me. I would anxiously run to the mailroom each day, hoping that she had written to me. I received fewer than a dozen letters from her that year.

Barbara returned to visit her parents and mine on a few occasions during my absence. They visited her on the Base once or twice. But visits from them were a rarity. As I had done in Turkey, I contacted the Red Cross, but they gave me no information except to say that she was OK. Barbara had become depressed and felt more isolated. Life for her in exile evolved solely around David once again. David was learning how to be resilient despite not having his father with him.

A week-long R&R (Rest and Recuperation) leave was permitted after serving in-country for six months. GI's would fly to Hawaii to meet their wives and children to enjoy a week of being together in a tropical paradise. Military personnel flew on government aircraft at no cost. Wives and children had to pay for commercial airfare. It would have stretched our budget, and as tempting as it was, I could not face the thought of being with Barbara and David for one week and then leave them again to return to Nam. They would have to return to Wurtsmith without me for another six months. I didn't think we could deal with saying goodbye again — I longed to be with them and never wanted to leave again.

I passed on Hawaii.

I needed something to keep occupied during my off time. Since I was in a communications squadron, I decided that I would become involved with the squadron's local MARS station in my spare time. MARS stands for the Military Affiliate Radio System. The local MARS station on the Base contacted civilian radio operators in the U.S. These civilian volunteers donated their time to provide telephone patches to their loved ones. This was the only communications line for GI's to use. I frequently hung out at the MARS Staton when I was not working at Peacock during the evening hours.

I often spent long nights waiting for the HAM Operators to connect with a civilian MARS operator who could patch me through to Barbara at Wurtsmith. I was able to connect quite a few times. Each call was limited by the need for others to also get through to their loved ones — in-depth conversations were not feasible. These phone calls required that only one person could talk and then had to say "Over." This indicated that the other person could speak, and then they had to say" Over '" meaning the first person could talk again.

This back and forth was tedious, and often connections were full of static. But, it certainly was better than no voice contact at all. Barbara never told me about the depression she was experiencing. Time allocations for these calls were limited. I was content just knowing that she and David were alright and that she loved me. I asked her to write to me more often.

Pleiku was popular with Army troops who would use on the Base to experience a real meal in the dining hall and a bunk and mattress and a shower for the night. The MARS station was furnished with a very comfortable waiting area and a private phone booth that ensured a feeling of privacy. However, conversations were not private because the system required the operators at the Base and the U.S. to listen to their conversations to switch from Send to Receive.

Working alongside the radio operators at the station as a volunteer, I heard the conversations also. It was not apparent to the GI making the call that we could listen to their conversations. On one occasion, we were almost brought to our knees with grief when we listened to an Army combat soldier tell his wife how much he loved her. Her response was, "Yeah, I just want you to know that I am fucking your best friend and want a divorce." The soldier went silent, and we could hear him sobbing while begging her to not leave him. She would listen to none of it, and she hung up the phone.

The young soldier sat for a minute or two in the phone booth, gathered his thoughts, and left the booth. He approached the operator's desk and said, "Thanks so much, guys, that was terrific." He turned and walked out of the MARS station. Our jaws dropped.

I thought of this often over the years and wonder what happened to this soldier. Did he make it out of Vietnam? Did he return home and salvage his marriage? Did he become one of the Vietnam vets who would commit suicide after discharge?

These long-distance MARS calls between us were usually concise and unfulfilling. I knew that my absence was taking a toll on Barbara and David but was powerless to do anything about it. Barbara seldom wrote to me, and there were months when I didn't hear from her. My parents would write about the visits they had with her and David. They were guarded in commenting about her well-being. That made me feel that they were hiding something, but they would say that they don't see her that often or some other inane reason when I asked them about this.

Living alone with his Mother for that year affected David. He felt abandoned. He relied on his innate resilience to cope with the terrible feeling of loss when I left him on the tarmac in the arms of his mother, grandfather, and grandmother. I sought to understand how David was coping with my absence in letters to my parents. Their response was that everything was OK. They skirted in-depth answers.

It was 1968, open discussions about the effect of the war on wives, children, and parents were not hot topics. Parents did not want to express their true feelings about their disdain for the war, especially in letters for fear of alarming those serving in Vietnam. Nor did they ask questions about what was really happening in Vietnam or what my living conditions were like. I often asked myself what I would say when I returned when people would question what it was like to be in Vietnam. I would tell them that it was a nightmare with no purpose and that our government was destroying the Vietnamese society for no valid reason. But, no one ever asked. I don't think families talked about the effect of war on children or on them. Perhaps they simply just viewed them as "collateral damage."

On February 24, 1968, the Tet Offensive ended as U.S. and South Vietnamese troops recaptured Hue's city. The U.S. government spun it as a victory for the United States and the South Vietnamese. Seven years later, the North Vietnamese Army entered Saigon, and the United States evacuated all military personnel from the country. The United States and the South Vietnamese Army had been ignominiously defeated. The citizens of the United States of America had supported a war for nothing.

Homeward Bound ▪ 1969

The twelve months I spent in Vietnam was about one thing—returning. It was the mission of every GI. No one I knew was proud to support the people of South Vietnam to make the world safe for democracy. We all knew that the Vietnamese people wanted to live in peace. The only thing we wanted was to return to the real world with our families. We fought to survive, not to win because we knew there was nothing to gain. It was the ultimate sham.

I counted the days until I would be released from duty at Pleiku. I finally received orders to depart Vietnam and return to Wurstmith AFB. The point of departure from Vietnam was at Cam Ranh Bay. I flew from Pleiku to Cam Ranh Bay and then waited in line for 16 hours for a flight to the U.S. When the aircraft took-off, every GI on board stood up and cheered. We were on our way home!

Upon arrival at the Seattle-Tacoma airport, I made a quick departure and a bee-line to the terminal without lingering on the tarmac. It was 1969, and the Vietnam War protesters were out in force. Some GI's who were walking to the terminal had been shot by snipers. We hurried. Welcome to the United States of America.

We entered the terminal and were told to "get a damn commercial airline ticket at the counter and go to wherever the hell you are supposed to go." After an overnight stay in Chicago, I took another flight to the Midland-Saginaw-Bay City (Michigan) airport.

I had called Barbara from San Francisco and again from Chicago and told her my arrival time for Bay City, Michigan. I had expected her to be joyous and relieved. Instead, she seemed unmoved and indifferent. I did not know what to expect. The flight from Chicago to Bay City was anxiety-ridden. My heart and my head were conflicted. Why was Barbara so un-emotional and unexcited to know I had returned? I dreamed about that phone call for 12 months. It was like waiting to be born again only to learn that you were dead. I should have known better.

I kept thinking that I would experience the same kind of rejection that the soldier whose phone conversation experienced with his wife at the MARS Station at Pleiku. My mind reeled with stories I just didn't want to envision.

I had no idea what had happened but did know that something was wrong. I knew that many GI's returned from Vietnam with shattered marriages. The separation was too painful for many couples to handle. I wondered if she had had an affair in my absence. I wondered what David had seen and what he knew. How would he have dealt with having another man in our home with his Mother? My mind reeled on that flight.

I flashed back to an earlier time when I had left Barbara to go to college. She drifted from me during that freshman year. When I returned, she announced that she had been sleeping with a guy she grew up with before I had met her. I was devastated. I could not handle the thought of her being intimate with someone other than me. It took me a full year to rid my mind of this. The feeling of betrayal that I felt has never escaped my psyche. Was I going to face a similar situation again? How would I know? Should I ask her if she was faithful to me while I was gone? Or should I just wait for the truth to reveal itself?

The flight to Bay City was uneventful. My mind was a wreck. I walked down the steps from the aircraft. Barbara and David were standing on the tarmac, ready to greet me. I ran toward them, and David ran to me. Barbara hugged me and kissed me. I held David in my arms. He held onto me tightly, as if he was afraid I would leave again without him. Barbara seemed to be numb. There was no emotion in her eyes.

I wondered if Barbara was in a state of despair. Was she a victim of the trauma that the war had inflicted on her? She seemed emotionally dead.

David was almost five years old and had not seen me for a year. Did he remember? Was he excited to be with his Dad again? I hoped that he still loved me and was happy that I was home. Not many questions were asked. It seemed more like going to wake than to a long-awaited reunion.

The 110-mile drive to the Base was just that. Nothing more. The Vietnam War ended for us not with joy but with a whimper.

We were united once again. The two-and-a-half-hour drive to the Base was surprisingly quiet. I was curious about how her life had been while I was gone. I simply could not understand why Barbara was so uncommunicative and had so few questions to ask me. It was a joy to be home. My eyes were filled with tears. I was grateful that I came home unharmed and not in a coffin. I had returned to the woman and son I loved at the Base at which I served before I left. I had two more years to serve on this second enlistment. We decided to terminate my enlistment at the eight-year point because we simply could not bear the agony of possible separation again.

Life at Wurtsmith AFB ▪ 1969

I took a 30-day leave when I returned, and during that time, we acclimated to living with each other again and became more open with each other. Barbara dispelled my fear that she had been unfaithful to me, and I told her that I was faithful to her. We felt the love we had for each other.

The first few weeks of being home with David and Barbara on the Base were adjustment periods. Nothing seemed to be real. I was mentally in Vietnam.

It was not possible to suddenly transition. The smell of Vietnam was embedded in my skin. The bathtub was full of a reddish tint for weeks. The red clay from Nam had permeated my clothes and my psyche.

I slept erratically. Every time I would hear a car door slam or aircraft from the Base taking off with their engines at full takeoff thrust, I would jump in my sleep. Sonic booms caused me to jump out of bed. Barbara continually asked me if I was alright.

Sex was unfulfilling for a while. I thought that when I returned, we both would act as if we were sex-starved. We were. But performing was difficult. Surprisingly, it required more practice and became fulfilling again after a few weeks. It was like the tourist in New York City who asked a pass-erby how to get to Carnegie Hall and was told, "Practice. Practice, Practice" — that was all it took. We had many practice sessions.

I was anxious to see how the town had grown, what new stores and restaurants had been opened, and learn what was new. Not much had happened in Oscoda. The town had not grown or changed.

We decided to take advantage of my 30-day leave to visit our parents in Aliquippa. I had not seen them for a year. David was glad to see his Grandparents with me at his side for a change. It made him feel complete. My parents and Barbara's parents were relieved to see me. They asked a few questions about Nam and what I did there. It seemed like they were trying to forget that I had been gone for a year. I felt that they did not want to know details, only that I returned — that mattered most to them. It was not the joyous reunion that I had anticipated. We spent four or five days with them and then returned to Oscoda to resume our life at Wurtsmith Air Force Base.

David and I had bonded again very quickly, and he was full of excitement to show me the things he was able to do. He took me into the woods, where we followed a stream. He was full of questions about nature. "What kind of tree is this?" "Where does the water come from, and where does it go?" "How long does it take a tree to grow a foot?" We saw frogs and tadpoles in the stream. David was fascinated with them and tried to catch them. "Hold my hand Daddy, so I can reach in to grab that frog without falling in the water." He scooped up a few tadpoles, and we talked about how they were hatched and how the bugs would be trying to get them so they could eat the frog eggs. We became great pals.

On one trip into the woods behind the Base, we came across a field littered with bones of all types… human bones, animal bones, and bones from unknown sources. I was at a loss to understand how they got there or what we should do about it. I explained to David that this must have been an Indian burial ground. It was once covered. It was exposed now because the ground soil was washed away by the stream many decades ago. That seemed to satisfy David's curiosity, and he grabbed a few bones to show his Mom and some of his playmates. We never learned the actual origin of these bones. I chose not to report it to the Air Force because I did not want to undergo the inevitable questioning that would follow. It remained an unsolved mystery that we often discussed many times after we left the Base.

David seemed to be a healthy boy who was well adjusted. His mother had taken great care of him once again in my absence. She was protective of him and preferred that I did not try to manage or discipline him. She unknowingly communicated to him and to me that she was his primary-parent and that she knew what was best for him.

I did not have the parenting skill or training to assert myself when I needed to do so. I had no practice at this or instruction on how to be a good parent. Regrettably, I viewed myself as an Air Force Air Traffic Controller. Barbara could attend to parental duties.

After my thirty-day leave, I reported to the 2030 Communications Squadron. I rejoined a lot of the controllers I had worked with previously. It was good to be back at a familiar Base that was not under attack. I was promoted to Technical Sargent and was awarded a Bronze Star for my Vietnam service at a monthly Commander's Call, a monthly meeting held by the Squadron Commander with all available personnel present. I was content for the next year and a half until I would be discharged.

David entered first grade in a very progressive school system on the cutting edge of elementary education. He loved every minute of it and would tell us exciting stories about what he was learning. Sadly, we would have to move him to another school after I was discharged. We had no idea what that experience would be like for him.

PART II

The Seventies

"The 'loser decade' that at first seemed nothing more than a breathing space between the high drama of the 1960s and whatever was coming next is beginning to reveal itself as a bigger time than we thought."

DAVID PATRICK MOYNIHAN

Kristi ▪ 1970

We decided to have another child before I left the Air Force. A few months later, Barbara told me she was pregnant. (All that practice paid off.) We would name the baby Kristi if Barbara delivered a girl. David was very excited, and we could feel our family growing in a different direction.

We waited patiently for the nine months to pass. I worked the standard three-shift rotation in the control tower, but we took advantage of any free time I had to visit the towns on Lake Huron's coast. David loved to see new places and loved the natural scenery of the coast. We drove to Aliquippa one long weekend to visit our parents so we could celebrate Barbara's pregnancy with them. They were excited to know that they would be grandparents again and hoped that Barbara would deliver a girl.

Kristi's birth in June 1970, just seven months before I accepted discharge after eight years of service in the Air Force, was a joyous and solitary experience for us. Our parents had been granted their wish for a granddaughter.

Barbara gave birth to her at the Wurtsmith Air Force Base Hospital. We were so excited when Barbara's water broke, and we rushed her to the hospital. David helped his mother get into the car, sat next to her, and caressed her belly to make her feel better. He wanted to be involved.

She was admitted, and David and I returned to our home to await the baby's birth. The Air Force did not permit family members to be in the delivery room or the patient's room. David and I waited patiently at home to receive notice that she had delivered the baby. We talked about what it would be like to have a new baby in the house and what David's life would be like with another sibling. He was very involved in the conversation, and I knew he was eager to welcome a new baby to the family.

The hospital called to tell us that Barbara had delivered a girl and that we could come over to the hospital to see Barbara and his new sister. We were not permitted in Barbara's room, so we had to stand outside the hospital at the window of her room. Barbara held Kristi in her arms, and David and I stood outside the window and looked at his mother and sister. She was wrapped in blankets in her Mother's arms. I took a few pictures through the glass window. One of them reflected me taking the picture outside the window with Barbra holding Kristi inside the window. Everyone loved that picture. David was thrilled and was anxious for his little sister to return home with his mother. We brought Barbara and Kristi home a few days later.

Kristi was a picture-perfect baby. She had blonde hair and brown eyes, coupled with a smile that just wowed everyone. David was fascinated with Kristi. He was six years old when she made her entrance into our lives, and David couldn't get enough of her. He was curious about everything she did and jumped right in to help Barbara care for her.

David asked his Mother, "If I touch her, will I hurt her? He had never held a baby before. His mother said, "Not if you are gentle, David."

"How much is gentle? Is it like you told me how to hold an egg, so it doesn't break?"

"That's just about right, honey. Here, hold her gently now."

David put his arm underneath Kristi. Barbara told him to put his other hand beneath Kristi's head because babies cannot lift their heads until they are a few months older. A big smile came over David's face as he held his sister. He was proud that he could do this without hurting her. Kristi looked up at David with her bright brown eyes and a big smile on her face. David instinctively bent his head down and kissed her on her cheek. Kristi smiled back and made a few cooing sounds. David was thrilled. He had a sister now and knew he was able to protect her.

In the months to follow, David and Kristi continued to bond. She caught on to almost everything immediately and soon started to define her personality. She showed an independent streak that followed her as she matured. David liked her rebelliousness and encouraged her to break the rules when she could.

Kristi had a foot abduction that required her to wear a Browns Bar when she was in her crib. Each morning we found her crawling around on the floor with the bar attached. We wondered how she was able to lift herself out of the crib. The bar was between her legs, so she had to pull herself over the crib. Then she had to land with her feet on the floor. We soon discovered that David had become her coach and was proud of it. "See what I taught Kristi? Don't be mad at me, please. She loves me to help her learn new things cause she catches on right away!"

We could only imagine what he would be teaching her as she continued to grow.

Civilian Life Nears ▪ 1971

Shortly before the end of my second term, I received a call from my commander at Pleiku, Major Orr. He identified himself as Lt. Colonel Orr.— he received the promotion I told him he would receive. I was working the midnight shift in the control tower and was thrilled to hear from him. He was calling from Korea and wanted to know if I would re-enlist for a third term. He told me how much he appreciated my service as the Information NCO at Pleiku and said he would help me advance in my career. I told him I appreciated his offer but could not bear having to leave my family again and planned to return to college. He said he understood and wished me future success.

I felt that my life had been constrained in the Air Force; the military's needs come first. I knew that with Lt. Colonel Orr's influence, I could attain more rapid career success. I also knew that I would face future overseas tours that would require me to move my family often. The thought of another unaccompanied tour was a risk I did not want to take.

Our family was now complete because we only wanted to have two children. In a few months, we would be leaving Wurtsmith AFB and Oscoda, Michigan. We were returning to the Real World.

I had been a model airman both on and off duty. Barbara and David had spent a total of two and a half years of the eight years that I was in the Air Force waiting for me to return. Kristi, still new to the world, was seven months old. Now we were free to live life together, not serve the country. We had given enough.

I received an Honorable Discharge from the United States Air Force in February 1971. W moved to Westminster College in New Wilmington, PA, where I had begun college as a freshman eight years previously. I had a degree to complete. I felt free. I was on my own, and my success would not be restrained by time-in-grade requirements before becoming eligible for a promotion. I would no longer be victimized by a sudden deployment to another war zone. Instead of the 'needs of the Air Force' coming first, I was now free to address our needs first.

The 'real world' as the Air Force called civilian life would soon be upon us.

David would not benefit from it.

The Reality of the Real World ▪ 1971

The 'real world' turned out to be very real—more real than we had anticipated.

New Wilmington, Pennsylvania, is a small town north of New Castle, only 50 miles from Aliquippa. It is a very rural town that is home to a Pennsylvania Dutch Community and Westminster College, a small liberal arts college. Bucolic best describes this part of Pennsylvania.

After a short visit with our parents in Aliquippa, I re-enrolled at Westminster College. I wanted to continue my education toward a degree in communications that I had begun eight years before enlisting in the Air Force. We moved into a rental farm home that was ideal for our needs. On Friday nights, we could hear the horses of Amish buggies clip-clopping down the street. Young bearded men drove the buggies. They wore their Amish black hats and drove their horse-driven buggy while their girlfriends sat the requisite distance away from their boyfriend after a Friday night out. Sometimes we could hear them giggling. Amish customs had changed little over the years, and we sometimes felt that we were part of another culture.

The farmhouse was home to fruit trees that produced cherries, peaches, and nuts and had a homemade maze that David and Kristi loved to get lost in. The autumn was spectacular on this property, with the oak trees, birch, and maple trees in full autumn splendor. The air was filled with the scent of their fallen leaves toasting on the ground. The large farm home was in reasonably good repair, but the owner paid an Amish craftsman to make needed improvements to the house. This craftsman would arrive in his horse-pulled buggy filled with his hand tools and would work all day without a break except for his lunch. He reconditioned the house so beautifully that the landlord decided to sell it. We moved to a brand new townhouse that was for rent in downtown New Wilmington. We missed the authenticity of the farmhouse.

I quickly learned that being a full-time college student, married with children, and the oldest student on the campus, was much different than I had imagined. I was not welcomed by other students and faculty members, and I initially wondered why. Then it dawned on me. I was a Vietnam Veteran on a college campus in 1971 at the height of the anti-war movement. No one on the campus harassed me or spit on me, as was common elsewhere — I was ignored. Professors did not make life tough on me; they routinely ignored me but gave me excellent grades just so they wouldn't have to deal with me. They seemed to be afraid of the only Vietnam Veteran and oldest married student on campus.

I decided to audit a speech course taught by a professor I admired eight years previously because I wanted to get a refresher. I took my original notes with me. To my amazement, he gave the same lecture that he delivered eight years prior — word for word. Now that he was a Ph.D., I assumed he would have some great new material. He didn't. He was intellectually lazy, as were most of the tenured faculty. And, I think they knew that I knew they were.

David completed his first grade of elementary school in Michigan. Their system of teaching was very modern. David was a star student there. Shortly after arriving in New Wilmington, David entered second grade at the local elementary school. Within a few weeks, we were called in to speak to the teacher. She informed us that David was more advanced than other second graders because of the progressive elementary school in Oscoda, MI, where he had completed first grade. The teacher advised that David be put back into first grade in New Wilmington and benefit from learning using their system. We felt he should stay in second grade. She said he was more advanced than other students in second grade and would have an advantage over them—making him feel out of place. We relented and permitted the teacher to put him back in first grade. David immediately lost interest in school, his grades fell, his self-esteem was damaged, and he never recovered. We saw a marked change in the little boy who had so much curiosity and excitement about being in school. It was one of the worst decisions we made and impacted David with contempt for the classroom and teachers. It followed him for the rest of his life.

It was not possible to live on a $175 a month GI Bill payment. Savings quickly dissipated. Attending a college where I was not welcomed was uncomfortable. I was sitting in the college library reading help wanted ads and found an opening for a representative for the Famous Writers School in Westport, Connecticut. I had taken their home study course in my free time in the Air Force and thought it was the best educational course I had ever taken. I felt qualified to explain it to prospective students. I applied, had an employment interview, and was accepted as a field representative for Famous Schools of Westport, Connecticut. My job was to interview prospective students who had contacted the school to determine if they had parental support and determination to complete a three-year study program. I received a recruitment fee for each student I recommended who stayed with the program. If they dropped out, my fee would be substantially charged back from my next paycheck. I had every incentive to recommend seriously interested students. My student's retention rates were among the highest in the country.

On my first day on the job, I earned over $500.00. I had been paid $438.00 a month as a Technical Sargeant in the Air Force. College professors did not earn $500.00 a week at that time. I thought, "What am I doing in college?" I finished that semester and dedicated myself to my new career in the business world.

I quickly became a sales-trainer because I had leadership and training skills. When the school president left to head up the oldest home study school in the United States, International Correspondence School, he invited me to join his management team. I did and quickly became, over the next 8 years, a division manager, regional manager, and national sales manager for the Eastern United States.

I became a success while Barbara, Kristi, and David awaited the company of a weekend husband and father because I traveled every week from Monday through Friday morning. Weekends were devoted to reports, phone calls, and finding the time to be with my family. I was never "present."

I became the absentee Father again. I thought that I was providing for my family by earning an excellent income. Instead, I inadvertently provided an incentive for my family to resent me and my 'quest for success.' And, in the process, ICS moved us three times. We lived in Buffalo, NY, Windsor, CT, and Merrimack, NH. I was on a fast track to more success with the company, but not with my family.

These changes had a direct impact on David. His lack of interest in school never changed. He no sooner had became accepted at a new school than we moved again. He felt that I had abandoned him. He made friends quickly but never acquired an interest in learning. He mentioned that his teacher asked all the students what their father's job was and told her that his Dad was a migrant worker. There was no need to wonder why.

David learned how to be resilient during these moves to new towns and school systems. He had no choice except to assimilate with his classmates. Still, his interest was not in assimilation — it was in their acceptance that he had no interest in making good grades. He knew how to simply do enough to get by with minimal effort. He became a below-average student with well above average capacity. The "real world" was becoming more real every day for all of us.

Merrimack, NH ▪ 1973-1979

David suffered during the '70s, and I didn't know it. I am sure that alcohol became his way of coping with the confusing messages he received from me. He became a victim of my desire to be part of the culture that defined the decade.

In my mind, I had achieved the material success I envisioned when I decided to leave the Air Force. I attained an above-average income in a career that gave me autonomy and an opportunity to influence others. It enabled us to purchase a home, drive a new automobile, and enjoy the American Dream. David was nine, and Kristi was three when we arrived in Merrimack. Now I wanted to enjoy the wild and crazy action that I had missed in the Air Force

We became more integrated and involved with our neighbors. David brought friends over more frequently. He entered junior high school during the time we spent in Merrimack. Kristi was in elementary school and was preoccupied with our neighbors, who had young girls her age, one of whom had horses that Kristi would help them care for and ride. Life seemed idyllic the first few years we lived in Merrimack but change rapidly.

Our neighborhood in Merrimack was an oasis of people in their late 20's and early 30, 's who loved the party scene. We missed the experiences most young adults crave in their 20's. We spent eight years in the Air Force living a non-social life. That would soon change.

Barbara and I discovered the uninhibited life-style of the seventies. We were not part of that life as an Air Force family and did everything we could to make up for those lost years. Alcohol, marijuana, free-sex, and rock and roll were inviting activities that excited us. Every weekend was party time—time to rock and roll while stoned and dirty dancing. We sang and danced along to Meatloaf tunes like Paradise by the Dashboard Light, Two Out of Three Ain't Bad, and Bat Out of Hell. Pool parties were always at night in an enclosed pool at another neighbor's house. It was titillating to be in the dark pool with five or six other couples groping private parts while wondering who we were groping. We were able to fit in… something we had no opportunity to do previously.

We thought that David and Kristi were unaware of what was going on. How naïve could we have been? David was old enough to know was going down and never mentioned a word to us. He was anxious to meet teenaged girls in the neighborhood that he could get to know really well. Kristi and her playmates were having fun acting like little girls act when their parents aren't around.

I had been assigned sales management responsibility for Maine, New Hampshire, Vermont, Massachusetts, and Connecticut. Merrimack was a central location. I took short overnight trips to meet and manage the sales representatives in those statesi, thereby allowing me to be home more often. Eventually, the need to travel each week increased but allowed me to be at home one or two nights during the week and weekends.

David and I had a strong bond, and he admired me and wanted to emulate me. He knew that his mother and I were smoking weed, drinking, and partying. Barbara had warned me the first time we tried grass that it would destroy our marriage. Still, the swinging neighborhood's excitement and close association with other women, who loved to smoke weed, soon became more exciting than anything she had ever experienced. Our libidos were freed. And so was David's.

David was fourteen years old and figured out what his mother and I were doing at all of those wild parties. He was attracted to other teenagers who enjoyed smoking weed and drinking. Barbara never shared this with me, and I regret that I was oblivious to David's activities. I had empowered Barbara to be in charge of the kids. She was very possessive of David. Her pride and protective attitude had been formed as his sole caretaker during the 18 months I was in Turkey and Vietnam. She disagreed with me when I tried to discipline him. I knew something was going on with him. I had mistakenly abdicated my parenting of him and Kristi to Barbara. Somehow, I had forgotten the values I learned under the Oak Tree.

David developed two or three close friends and occasionally brought them to the house. They seemed to me like good teenaged friends. David became interested in his first real girlfriend. He became rather possessive of her and ran into trouble when another boy his age tried to sway her away from David.

David would have none of this and confronted the boy. When the boy told David that she was now his girl, David reacted with fists. David was a strong boy and had lightning-fast reflexes and absolutely no fear of anyone. He was not afraid of getting hit by a bigger kid and laid into him with all he had— which was enough to put the boy in the hospital with a broken nose and facial bones. This seemed not to bother David and reinforced how resilient he was in dealing with new situations. David had also been hit but bounced back as if nothing had happened. I was on the road in Maine when this happened and learned about it when I returned. David was unaffected by the incident and was proud that the kid would not be standing between him and his girlfriend any longer. The boy's parents were not upset with David and did not demand an apology. It seemed as if they felt their son had learned a good lesson.

This reminded me of an episode I encountered as a 12-year-old boy when I defended myself from another kid trying to put me down because I was a small kid. When I told him to shut his mouth— he was so upset that he pulled a knife and tried to cut me. I sent him home with a bloody nose and a broken jaw. His father showed up that night and was ready to defend his son until I told him that the boy pulled a knife on me. He threw the kid into his car and drove off. By today's standards, this would have been a juvenile court event. But, it was the 1970's when boys often fought with no retribution. It was seen then as a boy becoming a man ritual.

I was pre-occupied with being known as the best sales manager in the company. I was not home frequently and when I was, I was not mentally present. I was still on the road, managing sales representatives. I relied on David's mother to handle the day to day lives of Kristi and David. That was a mistake because I did not give either of them the guidance and mentoring from the father they needed.

Ned

I met Ned in the 1970s when he applied for an admissions representative position with ICS (International Correspondence School) when managing a team of admission representatives in northern New England. Ned was living in Vermont and was an experienced salesperson. Our personalities hit it off immediately, and I hired him to be on my team. He was soon my top producing representative.

Over the years, our families spent many Thanksgivings together at Ned and his wife, Angie's rustic home nestled in the mountains of Vermont. They had three daughters, Laura, Michelle, and Bo. Their step-son, Sam, was older than his step-sisters. David and Sam would play catch in the yard and then kick around in the woods. Barbara and Angie would entertain the girls and play with them and their 160 pound Great Dane. From Ned's home, we could sit on the front porch and enjoy the views while reminiscing about sales and our sales careers. Vermont is a special place, unlike any other place I have been. Being there always a welcome respite from the rush of the "flatlanders," as Vermonters were fond of calling others who were not residents.

On one occasion, David and I traveled to Vermont at Ned's invitation to join him and his son, Sam, who was the same age as David, on one of their twice-yearly trips to a camp on a river thirty-five miles north of Montreal, famous for small-mouth bass fishing. Ned's avocation was fishing the river outside of the camp house he rented whenever he ventured there.

Every morning, we would awaken at 6:00 AM to set off in a small fishing boat to fish for small-mouthed bass. The river was the envy of bass fishermen from all over New England and that part of Canada. We trolled the river early in the morning and again in the late afternoon. David and Sam occasionally went fishing with us, but they spent most of their time searching for girls at other camps. They always returned with smiles on their faces.

I learned years later that the smiles were because they found girls who were high on pot.

After the trip ended, we bid Ned and Sam goodbye and returned to Merrimack. Little did I know that our paths would cross a few years later and would irrevocably change the course of our family's life and have a profound impact on David's.

Family Fun on the Road

I frequently took Barbara, David, and Kristi with me during the summer when they were not in school. We traveled throughout Maine, New Hampshire, Vermont, and Connecticut. I would check into a hotel from which I could meet my admission representatives. I would accompany them on their interviews with potential students and their parents. Afterward, I critiqued their interview and coached them. This one-on-one coaching was very beneficial to the representative. They were eager for me to observe them again. While I was coaching, Barbara and the kids would tour the area, check out the stores, and enjoy the motel's pool.

David and Kristi became accustomed to staying in hotels and to "life on the road." They became familiar with New England's geography and the differences in the way people lived in different states. Kristi acquired a real feel of direction and always was able to know where North was. One night she smelled smoke while we were sleeping and walked to the lobby to inform them. Then she calmly told us the hotel was on fire but that she had it under control. She also had a real knack for waking before we did and would walk to the restaurant to have breakfast in her pajamas. The hotel staff couldn't believe she was only four-years-old. We often laughed about that when we reminisced about those trips.

Kristi also had an intuitive sense of direction. She became an excellent navigator while we traveled, a skill that she retained as an adult.

I often discussed my career objectives with Barbara and the travel that it necessitated. She frequently told me that I spent more time with our kids than most fathers who were home every night. Even though she and the kids accompanied me often, she grew weary of the travel and the loneliness she felt when I was gonei. The excitement in the neighborhood and the parties held on the weekends seemed to satisfy her. At one point, she told me that she did not want me to travel but realized that she could not expect me to be responsible for her happiness. But by the end of the 1970s, after six years in Merrimack, I knew that I was not a role-model for David and Kristi. I began to look for opportunities to have a 9-5, weekend-free job in sales.

Family Tragedy

Tragedy struck one autumn morning at Ned and Angie's home. Ned had three young daughters. The youngest, Bo, was killed while waiting for a school bus with her sisters. The roads were icy that morning, and they waited patiently for the school bus to arrive. It was a few minutes late because of the ice. Suddenly a car came around a bend and slid sideways, hitting all three girls. Sam was already in high school and had been picked up by an earlier bus. Laura and Michelle suffered broken bones and internal injuries, but they lived. Bo, Ned's favorite and was killed. We drove to their home immediately to console and comfort them. Laura and Michelle were in shock from the trauma of the accident. Angie seemed outside of herself, and Ned grabbed the bourbon and remained in a stupor for almost a year.

We remained friends and continued to socialize with Ned and his family. They appreciated our friendship and looked forward to our visits — they had few other friends because they had moved so often. Ned suffered from Bo's death for the rest of his life.

They moved several times after Bo was killed — trying to escape the accident scene and the pain that accompanied it. They finally moved into a home on the top of a mountain near Okemo, Vt. The view was spectacular, and the beauty of the hills and streams surrounding the mountain were breathtaking. I can still smell the autumn leaves and the scent of mountain air—crisp and invigorating.

Ned was a dog lover, and Great Danes were his favorite breed. They became part of the family. Danes are not known for long lives, and the newest member of the family was Baron. It was a real treat to see the kids playing with this giant brown and black dog, who was almost the size of a pony. Bo loved Baron, so Ned and the family felt that Baron was the part of Bo that lived on. Baron brought them comfort.

Over the years, David and Kristi, and Barbara and I spent many Thanksgivings together at Ned and his wife, Angie's home nestled in the mountains of Vermont. Ned and I sat on their front porch and relished the views while reminiscing about sales and our sales careers. Barbara and Angie would entertain their daughters. David would pal around with Sam. Those Thanksgivings with them were always special to us. They had become our extended family.

Reflections

As the 70s drew to a close, I envisioned a new beginning for our family in the '80s. New decades often caused me to reflect on how past experiences could influence future events in my life. My thoughts turned to my childhood and the lessons I learned from my parents. Would the values I discovered sitting under the oak tree and the experiences hold fast? Would the experiences I had with my parents influence the relationship I would have with David and Kristi as we entered the 80s and beyond?

My mother, Margaret Harrison Greene, was called Margie by all of those who knew her well. It was a term of endearment that she loved. She was the youngest of five children — one sister and four brothers — born and raised in Sewickley, Pennsylvania, a short drive from downtown Pittsburgh. Sewickley prided itself on its wealthy residents who lived in Sewickley Heights. — an exclusive area of mansions owned by the ultra-wealthy industrialists like Andrew Carnegie, Thomas Mellon, Charles Schwab, and George Westinghouse.

Margie's father, Charles Harrison, was employed as a chauffeur for these magnets of industry. He had immigrated from England, where he became a skilled chauffeur. He became a trusted advisor to these scions of the industry in matters of household help. When he learned that a Nanny was needed for the family, he recommended his daughter, Margie. In her early twenties, she was chosen as a Nanny for the upper-class children and accompanied them to their summer homes on Cape Cod. Margie became a companion for her aging clients in later years when they needed someone to watch over them each night. Mom slept in an adjoining bedroom to comfort them as their personal attendant. She continued to serve succeeding generations of those families until she was in her 70's.

My Mother and Father met in a speakeasy during prohibition in the 1930s. She was a diminutive lady and had stunning blue eyes. She wore her blond hair rolled over her ears — the style of forward-thinking women at that time. She had a unique sense of humor and enjoyed telling slightly ris-que jokes and sayings like, "Between dishes and douches, I'm in hot water all the time." She kept every party and social gathering interesting. She and my father fell in love dancing the Charleston during the Roaring Twenties. She was a real flapper, and Dad loved to dance. All eyes were on them.

My father was a clothes horse. He wore a suit and tie with a pocket-silk in his jacket pocket and seldom wore casual clothes. He was a student at the Art Institute of Pittsburgh. He sported a well-groomed mustache with slightly rolled tips — a short version of a handlebar mustache, but not Dali-esque. How could they not be attracted to each other? It was inevitable that they would be married after dating for a few years.

I was born two years after their marriage. Dad worked for a few years in the American Bridge Company's payroll department in Ambridge, Pennsylvania, a town across the Ohio River from Aliquippa. He had his eyes on a bigger paycheck and left his payroll clerk job to become a sales-man. He knew successful salesmen who were earning big commissions, and he wanted a taste of real money. He was an immediate success and earned enough to move from their apartment into their first and only home on Golf Course Road in Aliquippa.

Mother became a dedicated housewife. Her first priority was tak-ing care of me. Dad's sales territory was from Maine to Florida, selling Topper Magazine to dairy farmers. Topper Magazine was a forerunner to Prevention Magazine. It contained articles on family life, health, and nutri-tion. Dairy farmers gave it to their milkmen to distribute to their customers to help them earn their loyalty. The magazine was an excellent prospecting tool for the milkmen to give to new families on their route to increase their business. Dad was usually gone for four or five days at a time. Mom and I traveled up and down the east coast with him occasionally.

We would wait for him in the car while he met with prospective dairy owners. On one occasion, Mom and I were sitting in the car waiting for him when we saw him rushing out of the owner's office with the owner chasing him. Dad jumped in the car and quickly drove off. Mom was alarmed and said, "Raymond, what is going on?" Dad drove a mile or so and said, "I waited for the receptionist to tell me to go into the owner's office. He was reading a document on his desk when I entered. After a few seconds, he looked up and said to me, "Oh no, another damn salesman." Dad asked the owner why he thought he was a salesman, and the owner said, "You have a briefcase, don't you?" Dad said, How do you know that I am not an attorney bringing you a check for $50,000? But now you will never know". He abruptly turned and left the office.

The owner was stunned and chased Dad. Mom and Dad and I could not stop laughing as Dad drove away. At the same time, the owner stood in the dust, yelling, "Come back! Come back!" Dad knew the owner would never again assume anything about someone with a suit and a briefcase. As we traveled from one dairy farm to the next, Dad would practice his presentation with my mom and me. This was great fun, and we delighted in giving Dad objections that he would have to overcome. I received my early education in sales that served me well in years to come.

One winter in 1951, we were riding with Dad in the South, and his next call was near Miami. It was Christmas Eve, and Dad checked into the White House Hotel. Dad hired a man to wear a Santa Claus suit and to come into our room at 3:00 AM to put presents under a little tree that the hotel loaned to us. I was absolutely thrilled to wake up (after being nudged by Dad) to see Santa leaving our room. I remember the presents Santa brought to me — a cowboy hat, leg chaps, cowboy boots, and a toy six-shooter in a holster. Traveling with Dad ended when I entered first grade. Dad was so successful selling the magazine that the company could not meet production and eventually went out of business. Mom and Dad had invested in the company. They lost all of their money. Dad was not deterred and found other companies to represent. He continued to earn a living through his sales skills. His territories remained large, and he had to travel for one or two weeks at a time.

Mom and I spent many weeks just waiting for Dad to return. We would count the days until he returned. Telephone calls to another state were called 'long-distance calls' and were very expensive, and the charges had to be reversed to our home phone bill. The operator would say, "I have a collect call from Raymond. Will you accept the charges?" Dad did not call every day, but he would call when he knew what day he would return. We eagerly waited for his call.

Mom was my primary care-giver and spent hours reading to me while Dad was gone. I was moved by her tear-filled eyes when she read emotionally moving passages. She gave me a love of reading that has inspired much of my life. She was a very loving mom devoted to me and seldom had to discipline me. But when I flagrantly disobeyed, she was swift to tell me that I would have to explain my disobedience to Dad when he returned. That usually got my attention and inspired me to shape up — fast.

One Sunday morning, before Dad was ready to leave on another trip, he came to hug me and give me a kiss. I was 10 years old. He held me in his arms and kissed me. I didn't want him to leave and grabbed hold of him with all my strength, with tears rolling down my cheeks, and pleaded with him not to leave again. "Daddy, please don't go. Mom and I don't want to be alone again. We miss you too much. Please don't go." He held me and looked me straight in the eye with tears pouring down his face and said, "Harrison, I promise this will be my last trip away from you and your Mother. I will never leave you again." He kept his word.

Dad knew the owner of a local dairyman, Roy Sutherland, who he met when selling Topper Magazine. He let Roy know that he had decided to come off the road and persuaded Roy to represent the dairy as the public relations director. Roy liked Dad's speaking ability (he had a deep, commanding voice and an ability to be empathic with others). Roy envisioned Dad as the spokesman for the dairy and offered Dad a position as the public relations director.

Dad asked Roy if he could introduce me to him to inspire me by coaching me to become financially successful. Roy was glad to meet with me and told me, "Harrison, the secret to financial success is to save ten-percent of every penny you earn." I wish I had listened to his advice.

One of the things Dad did was to show movies about the benefits of milk to students in the schools in and around Aliquippa. He encouraged them to drink milk to build healthy bodies. The kids loved him and received rave reviews from the Principals of the schools. The kids were impressed with his appearance and speaking ability and thought it was really cool that he was my Dad. Roy eventually sold the dairy. Dad began a search for another local area sales job.

Dad worked for a variety of different companies that needed an excellent salesman over the years. He sold ads to local businesses for the local newspaper and bronze memorial markers for a cemetery. He became an account executive at an advertising agency. Dad stayed true to his promise and looked for sales jobs that did not require travel. I admired him for his integrity and his ability to always find a way to support us.

My mother showed me how to be caring, considerate, and empathic. Empathy became a value I wanted to help frame decisions I would make in the future. But, as a youngster, I had an opportunity to be empathic, caring, and considerate sooner than I expected. I gave up my bedroom when I was twelve so that Grandma and Grandpa Harrison could live with us. I slept on the living room couch. They became incapable of caring for themselves. Mom assumed responsibility for letting her mother and father live with us when they were in their 80s. Her siblings didn't offer to help out, which speaks volumes about how much they cared about their mother and father.

Mom worked as a dry cleaning attendant to support us when Dad was not receiving enough commission checks — he was not a real hustler. Traveling salesmen paid their own expenses and worked on a commission basis. Dad sold until he met our basic living standard, and often it was not enough. He was tired of traveling and hustling for a paycheck. He longed for a salaried job with a prestigious company that would befit his demeanor. That job would materialize a few years later.

Grandma was blind, had one glass eye, and wore a wig. Grandpa was the epitome of a proper English Gentleman but suffered from dementia. I took care of Grandma and Grandpa when Mom worked at the dry cleaner shop. I learned how to help Grandma on and off the potty chair. I learned how to remove and clean her glass eye. Mom was too squeamish to do it, Grandma was always concerned about her appearance and asked me to make sure her wig was placed correctly. I entertained Grandma and

Grandpa in what was supposed to be my bedroom by hiding from under the bed, and grabbingGrandpa by his ankles, surprising him. He and grandma got a good laugh out of my pranks. I loved them dearly and wanted to protect them when my mom could not be there. Mom counted on me and was proud that I was willing to help.

Grandma was a devout Catholic and the local priest, Father Thomas, visited her once a month to give her communion. He was a middle-aged man who seemed to want to be around me when he visited Grandma. It seemed to me kind of weird when Father Thomas would touch my shoulder and get very close to my face to tell me what a fine young man I was. I felt very uncomfortable with this and told mother that I did not want to be around him because he was weird. She replied, "Harrison, Father Thomas has been anointed by God. You should not feel that way about him." I made it a point to be somewhere else when Father Thomas visited Grandma.

I know that the lessons I learned were valuable ones. In the years to come, I tried to impart the value of caring for others and having empathy for older people to David and Kristi. Grandma and Grandpa both passed away in the late 1950s. Mom was now free to devote her energy to being a great mother and a loving wife. But not for long.

In the 60s, my father's sister, Jessie, could not take care of the home she lived in all of her life with her parents and her twin sister, Bessie. Bessie was the dominant twin, and Jessie followed along. Grandma and Grandpa Greene both passed away within a year or two in the mid-60s, and Bessie died shortly after that, so Jessie had nowhere to go except to live with us. So, my mother's respite from caring for others took on a new dimension when Jessie moved into my bedroom. I was in my mid-teens and was happy to give up my room again. I really loved Aunt Jessie and was happy to help her. She was a kind woman and had a great sense of humor. I was fascinated when she told me she could play the piano by ear.

Mother was full of resentment that once again, she did not have the house to herself. Mom was worn out, taking care of others. Since Jessie was physically capable of taking care of herself, she ignored Jessie most of the time. My father felt trapped and did not know how to accommodate

Jessie's need to be part of the family while supporting my mother's need for autonomy. So, Jessie stayed in her room for over three years. Jessie knew that my mother did not welcome her at all. Mom insisted that Jessie stay out of her kitchen and prepared trays for Jessie's meals. I could not tolerate my parents' inability to deal with this situation. This became a contentious situation and was a contributing factor in my feeling of disrespect for my father's inability to provide the family with leadership. I was glad to graduate from college and live away from home.

When I was stationed in Turkey in 1964, Mom and Dad put Jessie in a nursing home that was newly built and just a few hundred yards from their house. Barbara took Jessie clothes shopping and wanted to make Jessie feel that she was cared about. Barbara was instrumental in making the nursing home an option for Jessie when she could no longer care for herself. Jessie died while I was in Turkey, and Barbara helped arrange her funeral. I was sad that I was not there and very thankful that Barbara did so much for Jessie.

Once again, in the 70s, my parents had the house to themselves for a few years. Their Cape Cod style home was graced with an acre and half of beautiful trees. There was a fishpond in the back yard. Their property was the neighborhood's envy, with its long driveway leading to a separate garage behind the house. A hand made brick wall separated the driveway from the back yard. The backyard's focal point was the 350-year-old oak tree that majestically dominated and seemed to protect the family. It was a beautiful, well-maintained home that was their pride and joy.

My father was diagnosed with lung cancer in 1975. His condition worsened slowly while Mom struggled to help him. I regret that I was unable to be there for him during those two years. Barbara and I and the kids visited him a few times but could not stay for longer than a few days.. Fortunately, Mom and Dad traveled to Wurtsmith to visit us before Dad became too sick to travel. During one of their visits, I suggested to Dad that we drive to Boston to visit the Boston Museum of Fine Arts. He was excited because he knew that there were several Rembrandt works on display. We drove to Boston and arrived at the Museum. Dad could hardly walk up to the long flight of stairs leading into the Museum. He was exhausted and could not breathe well. He got his strength back after fifteen minutes or so. We spent an hour or two looking at the Rembrandt'art (Dad's favorite)s and other works by Renaissance painters that he admired. He knew he reached the limit of his energy during those two hours and wanted to get back to our house so he could rest. I grieve that I could not have been with him more when he was end-stage.

Dad suffered in his final year and finally died in 1977. Barbara, David, and Kristi and I flew to Pittsburgh to be with my Mom. Dad had donated his body to the University of Pittsburgh medical school, so there was no funeral. Mom arranged a Memorial Service that was attended by over fifty business people, friends, and relatives. Ron, my childhood friend, had become a preacher and Dad wanted Ron to conduct the service. The memorial service was not pretentious. I admired Dad's humanitarianism by donating his body to science so medical researchers and students could increase their knowledge.

Mother could no longer maintain the property and the house by herself after my father died. Barbara and I convinced her to move to Nashua, NH, twenty minutes from our home in Merrimack. She was not hesitant and viewed this as an opportunity to start out again on her own in an apartment that she could easily manage and give her a sense of security. She seemed excited to know that she could live independently without attending to others' needs.

Barbara flew to Aliquippa to help her empty the house, attend to the property, and arrange the details of hiring a moving company. Her help provided just the right amount of support my Mother needed and made Mom's relocation much more comfortable.

I feel grateful for these childhood experiences. They framed my inner core and let me understand what I needed to teach my children.

Future decades would reveal how well I succeeded.

PART III

The Eighties

"*Everything in everybody's life is ... significant.
And everybody is alert, watching for the meanings.
And the vibrations. There is no end of vibrations.*"

TOM WOLFE

Eyes Wide Closed ▪ 1980

It was a Sunday afternoon in 1980 when I saw a help-wanted ad in the Boston Globe for a College Sales Manager. I was intrigued and interested. What kind of college could be looking for a sales manager? Central New England College was in Worcester, MA. It was struggling to survive and had appointed a results-oriented president. He knew that profit-making technical schools used aggressive sales and marketing methods unheard of by traditional non-profit colleges.

I responded to the ad and was invited to an interview with the president. He was an entrepreneur who had spotted an opportunity to turn around a struggling college. I explained that I was an expert at using non-traditional and contrarian enrollment methods to differentiate the college and increase enrollment. After several interviews, he offered me a position as Director of Admissions. The vision I told him I had would save the college from closure, the board would be thrilled, and he would become famous. I accepted the position, and within a few months, we moved to Westborough, a suburb of Worcester.

The Greene family was excited. A new house with a pool. A new school system that had rave revues. We had arrived in suburbia, and Barbara, David, Kristi, and I were thrilled. I now had an executive-level job at a local college that did not require travel. This is what we had sacrificed so much for, and now we had it — a normal life.

Since my mother lived in Nashua, a 60-minute drive from Westborough, we asked her if she would like to live with us in our new four-bedroom home. She was delighted to be part of our family, and we were grateful that she was able to live with her grandchildren and be part of their lives. The move from Nashua to Merrimack was easy.

Mom had her own bedroom in our new home and spent hours there reading, sewing, and talking to Kristi. She enjoyed telling Kristi stories about her childhood, and Kristi was eager to know more about her Grandmother's life. Kristi was twelve, and Grandma kept her intrigued. But as the months passed by, Kristi devoted most of her time to her school mates.

Margie was thrilled to have the opportunity to babysit for us when we wanted to visit friends or take weekend trips by ourselves. It was almost as if she was back in Sewickley Heights, serving as a companion again. David and Kristi liked her because she was funny and would joke with them. This was the first time both of them had really gotten to know a grandparent and giggled at her because she seemed "a bit old-fashioned." They learned to respect her despite some of her idiosyncrasies. She remained with us until her death from lung cancer in 1982.

We held a public viewing service at a local funeral home. The service was attended by a few of the friends' Mom made in Westborough. Unfortunately, her friends from Aliquippa could not make the trip to Westborough before the funeral.

We buried Mother at the town cemetery in a private ceremony presided by a minister from the Unitarian Universalist Church where we were members. David, Kristi, and Barbara and I said our final goodbyes to Grandma Greene. David would visit her gravesite frequently. He loved her.

Everyone enjoyed life in Westborough, but for David, there was one missing ingredient — acceptance. He was now thrown into a high school that was focused on college-bound students. David had the intellectual capacity to succeed in high school. Still, he did not have the ambition to become a hit with college-bound students. So, he resorted to the only tactic he knew to fit in. He became the "Fonzie" of the high school. His friends became those who did not have college-bound aspirations. They were interested in Parties, Alcohol, Drugs, Girls, and Sex. David knew how to become a leader. This was how he gained acceptance. They were not punks, not prone to juvenile delinquency or unlawful acts except for marijuana and alcohol. They were good kids who had the wrong motivations and weak guidance. They accepted David. He was the one everyone liked. David was in his element.

David was a hit with these friends but not with his teachers, who tried to ignore him. I would often drive him to school on my way to the college and drop him off in front of the school where kids congregated in the morning. I had no knowledge that these kids were lighting up joints before going into the building. The teachers were very aware of this but did nothing to stop it. Perhaps they felt weed kept the troublemakers like David subdued. I was angry at myself for not recognizing this at the time.

David's mother accepted him and gave him almost complete freedom to do what he wanted. She was preoccupied with Kristi's education and social life. She became friends with other mothers in Westborough while I was busy building revenue so a college could survive. We were "living the dream" but not focusing on the right kind of dreaming for David or Kristi. Our eyes were wide closed.

Resilience Is Reinforced ▪ 1981

David learned about the great equalizers… marijuana and alcohol when he was twelve when we lived in Merrimack. David knew he could become very popular by being the 'bad boy" after moving to Westborough. He sought out cliques that drank beer and liked reefers — the partiers and non-achievers. David was their hero. The girls in this clique were drawn to him. His charisma attracted both boys and girls who wanted to party with him. His best friend's father was a police officer and had large ornate vases full of confiscated marijuana and cocaine in their house. It was a party-lovers dream come true.

Even at a young age, David could conceal his drinking and smoking very well. In fact, he could be cold stone drunk at 5am and sober-like by 10am. This resilience fooled his mother and me for a long time.

I was not a strict parent because I knew Barbara would not back me up. She wanted to manage his activities. I relied on her to parent and discipline David and his sister. It was a mistake that David capitalized on. His Mother was sympathetically blind to David's behavior. After all, he was her baby. She carried him and gave birth to him when I was in the Air Force in Turkey and raised him while I was in Vietnam. I was never able to convince her that David had serious problems once I became aware of them.

I became aware of the extent of David's behavior when David was 16-years old, and I was driving on the road leading to our house. Ahead of me, I saw someone staggering and trying to hitchhike a ride. As I approached closer, I knew that it was David. I stopped, and he got into the car. His speech was slurred. He was drunk. I wanted to know where he had been drinking. He would not tell me. Before I could probe further, we were home. He drunkenly exited the car, and I escorted him up the steps to the front door. His mother feigned shock to see David like this.

I was simultaneously furious and saddened by his drunkenness. His mother said nothing. I grabbed him and shoved him into the bathroom, and told him to get into the shower. When he resisted, I jumped in the shower and pulled him in with me. He could hardly stand as I ran cold water full force on him, hoping to sober him up. He tried to resist, but I forced him to stand there in the shower with me. After five minutes or so, I pushed him out.

He hurriedly staggered naked into his bedroom and fell into bed. He was sleeping and snoring within seconds. His mother was angry at me for being "so rough on him."

I had no idea whether I did the right thing or not. I was on the verge of tears. Barbara and I said very little, as I recall. We did confine him to the house for a period, but I don't remember how long.

Later, she accused me of being a father who wanted David to be a "perfect little boy like the little Lord Fauntleroy that you were."

She should have accused me of being an absentee father who abdicated my role to a mother who could not accept the reality that her son had a problem. She would have been accurate on both counts.

David felt vindicated. His resilience was reinforced to guide him again.

I was distraught and knew we must take further action.

Barbara and I discussed what we should do about this drunken episode. She attributed his behavior as something that all teenagers go through in high school. I knew that there was more to it than just teenaged behavior.

I recalled that David's interest in applying himself to his education had diminished each year since he was in the second grade. I knew that he was demoralized and never recovered when he was put back into the first grade. He lost interest in his education from that point and only did enough each school year to pass into the next year.

A few months after we moved to Westborough, David drove to Merrimack to visit the friends he missed. They celebrated their reunion by driving around town smoking week and guzzling beer. The police apprehended them and took them to the police station. We received a phone call from the Merrimack police department informing us that they were not pressing charges but that we had to take him home. The Chief knew David and liked him and decided to give him a break. We thanked the Chief for giving David a break. The ride home was not a fun trip for David. David had driven his mother's car to Merrimack, and she drove it home while David rode with me. He did not linger in the car when we arrived and was confined to his room for two weeks unless he was at school.

These experiences in Merrimack and in Westborough seemed to have become his identity. I wanted to get at the root cause of his behavior made an appointment with a well known Boston psychiatrist, who was recommended. When we arrived, the psychiatrist talked to Barbara and me first. I explained my concern about David's use of alcohol and his errant behavior, lack of interest in school, and ambition to prepare for the future. I explained David's childhood to provide some background. He said he would meet with us again after he spoke with David. We waited in the waiting room while the psychiatrist met with David privately for 15 or 20 minutes.

When he finished his brief fifteen-minute session with David, the psychiatrist told David to wait in the waiting room and then met privately with us. He informed us that "David is exhibiting behavior very typical of a teenager, and he will grow out of it. No further visits are necessary." My immediate thought was, not with you, that's for sure.

We drove home. David's mother had expressed a 'See, I told you' attitude. David was ok, and we were not to worry.

This advice was wrong. I knew it. David's Mother believed he would outgrow it. I doubted that he would.

David felt vindicated.

Resilience showed its face again.

Outward Bound ▪ 1982

David loved the outdoors. He never forgot the experiences we had in the woods at Wurtsmith AFB. Oscoda, Michigan is famous for camping, rafting, nature walks, lumberjack competitions, and canoeing. David was intrigued by all of nature and loved the nature classes he had in elementary school.

I knew that the psychiatrist had no clue about the severity of the problems plaguing his mind. I read about the Outward Bound program and thought it might be ideal for him. The program featured all-outdoor experiences over The Appalachian Mountains and through the lakes and rivers for 15 days traveling through Maine's unforgettable wilderness with male and female students his age. He was enthusiastic and excited about the adventure. The program included a two-day solo experience on the bank of a secluded lake. He would be dropped off early in the morning and picked up late in the afternoon the next day. He was incredibly stoked about that.

Barbara and I drove him to the starting point. He was fully equipped with all of the camping gear he needed and eagerly said goodbye to us — he couldn't wait to meet the other students. We told him we would be anxious to see him when we picked him up. We hugged and kissed and wished him a safe and fun trip. We would not hear from him during the trip unless there was an emergency.

Fifteen days later, we returned to the Outward Bound site in Maine to pick him up. We never expected what we saw. David looked like a stranger. His hair was all over his head and looked like it had not been washed in two weeks. He had a beard, and his clothes were filthy. We expected that he would look like he had been in the woods for two weeks but never expected to see him feeling so mentally and physically wrecked. He was not happy and was very non-communicative. We wondered what was wrong with him but did not barrage him with questions. We felt he needed some time to readjust to civilized life.

The ride home was worrisome. When we arrived, he took his gear, threw it in the garage, and went into his bedroom. He was exhausted. He awakened the next morning and had breakfast with us. His story of the adventure was not encouraging.

I asked him why he seemed so unhappy and depressed when we picked him up. David said that the experience was a good one. He loved the mountains and camping out each night. But he did not feel that it was a positive learning experience.

The eight other members of his team were college-bound kids. They viewed the Outward Bound experience as a blow out party experience in the woods before entering college in the autumn. Since David was not interested in college, he was viewed as an outlier. But he found a couple of the girls on the team who were attracted to him — and they carried an ample supply of weed with them. David lit up with them in more than one way. He said he did not get much sleep during most nights and that everyone was sluggish the next day.

His team was not adequately monitored by the Outward Bound leaders. They accompanied them on the wilderness adventure, but they turned their heads away from the partying each night. They had their own parties.

David loved the solo part of the trip. He was taken to an isolated island to reflect on nature while fending for himself, isolated from everyone. While one of the leaders checked on him during the day, they did not communicate.

David felt that the seclusion gave him time to realize that he loved the mountains and camping alone. It was a meditative experience for him. I asked him why he seemed so despondent when we picked him up. He said he was physically and mentally exhausted and confused and just wanted to be left alone for a while.

I could tell that he struggled to understand himself better and hoped that he would discover a way to feel accepted without relying on alcohol and drugs.

The Pattern Is Established

There had been too many near-death experiences in his life. His early growth was fueled by a concussion when he was hit full force on his head by a baseball bat when he was ten. He fell 80 ft. out of a tree when he was twelve, suffering another concussion and broken bones. A motorcycle accident when he was seventeen landed both him and his girlfriend in the hospital. She was not severely injured. He was hospitalized for days while he recovered from another concussion, broken bones, and facial lacerations.

Yet he was resilient and recovered as if nothing had happened at all. These early life experiences all resulted in brain concussions. They were the results of a fearless boy. He loved to take risks and believed he could always get away with it because he knew he was resilient enough to overcome anything.

A motorcycle accident at age 17 foreshadowed another more deeply-rooted problem. He was drunk when he careened off the road with a girlfriend and landed in a wooded marshland. An ambulance took them to the University of Massachusetts emergency room. Her parents understood and held no grudge, threatened no legal action, and were glad their daughter only had a broken ankle. His mother and I were afraid he might not survive because we were told that the doctors were uncertain about his condition. Many hours later, they informed us that he would continue to be evaluated and kept in the hospital. He was treated for broken bones in his arm and leg, facial lacerations, and a concussion.

David walked out of the hospital three days later. His arm in a cast and he had a brace on his leg. He acted as if nothing had happened. His resilience had carried him through another episode.

But, the nagging feeling that something was seriously wrong plagued me. Everyone passed off his being drunk at 17 as a lousy thing that kids do. I was concerned about the alcohol and his lack of interest in school and the group of teenagers with whom he was associating.

When David showed no interest in his future, I told him that he had three choices when he graduated from high school. He could go to college, and I would help pay for it —David felt his high school education was a joke and his interest in college was non-existent. Second, he could join the military, or a third option, get a job and pay rent if he wanted to live at home. He said he would enlist in the Air Force after graduating from high school, just like I did when I could not afford to stay in college.

Into Adult Life

During high school, David was intimately involved with many girls. He had acquired the reputation of being a true Casanova. Aside from affairs with high school girls, David had a long-running sexual relationship with a beautiful young married woman. She worked with his mother in a gift shop. He would meet Lindsay at the gift shop, and they would put the "Closed until _____ " sign on the door and would have sex in the back-room of the shop. David's mother knew about this but was good friends with Lindsay, who claimed she loved David. When Lindsay was not working, they satisfied their passion at a local motel. This affair became so intense that Lindsay's husband moved them to another town in another state. Lindsay begged David to move to her new home town, but David refused.

David soon accepted that Lindsay was gone, although he told me years later that he missed her unbridled passion. David started to date Janey, one of his classmates, during his senior year. She was a sweet, bashful girl. Janey was thin without appearing to be skinny and was enamored with David's charm and decisiveness. Right before he graduated, he learned that she was pregnant. She and David decided on her parent's and his mother's advice to have an abortion.

I told David that this decision was Janey's and that he needed to support her wishes if he loved her. He said that they were in love with each other, but they did not want a child at their age. I told him that I understood.

David's mother took Janey and her mother to a Planned Parenthood facility in Boston for the procedure. It was successful. Janey had no medical problems afterward.

After graduation from high school, David enlisted in the Air Force and told us that he would return to marry Janey. He said he would take her with him to wherever he was assigned.

His mother was relieved and, to my surprise, did not seem bothered that David was leaving home. Barbara found it convenient that David would not be around because of circumstances that David was unaware.

David's departure for Air Force Basic Training signaled me that this was the harbinger of more to come.

The Adult Rated Camping Trip

Ned slowly recovered from Bo's death. He never had a monogamous marriage with Angie and relieved his pain with alcohol and women. He was trying to forget his grief by frequent trips to the fishing camp in Canada with a newly found paramour named Fern.

Fern was a former nun who left the convent after 20 years. She could not stand having to remain celibate while living a life of seclusion while honoring her vows of poverty. She wanted to be free and had lost faith in Catholicism. She met Ned during an employment interview for a job with the sales organization that Ned managed after he returned to work a few months after Bo's death. Fern and Ned began a sexual relationship that lasted for a few years. He often took her to the fishing camp, and on one of these trips, he invited Barbara and me to join them.

When we arrived at the camp, Barbara and Fern were immediately sexually attracted to each other. Fern loved to be the center of attention and was very aggressive in her pursuit of sex with women. Her sexuality was palpable. Barbara was immediately attracted to Fern. It was apparent that both she and Fern were looking for more than friendship.

We arrived at the camp late in the afternoon, and after small talk over dinner that we prepared, Ned broke out the bourbon, and Barbara broke out the weed. Ned and Fern were in one bedroom in a few hours, and Barbara and I were in another. Everyone returned to the kitchen when they were finished with what was Act One. The munchies prevailed.— the bourbon and pot were enjoyed by everyone. Fern and Barbara sat together, murmuring quietly, smoking a joint. Ned and I were telling each other jokes when suddenly they returned to the bedroom and shut the door. Ned and I could hear their ecstatic and erotic screams and sex talk that seemed to go on for hours. We just looked at each other. I said, "I am afraid they have awakened their sexuality and ignited a flame that will never be extinguished." It never was. The camping trip was the beginning of an open marriage.

Fern became a frequent visitor to our home in the months to come and rented my mother's former bedroom while looking for a new home in Saratoga Springs,

David had no knowledge of this because he and Janey were In Arizona. Kristi was in grade school in Westborough and was not aware of her mother and Fern's affair. Barbara told Kristi that Fern would temporarily be with us while Fern found a job and a home in Saratoga Springs.

Abandonment and Rage ▪ 1983

I awakened one morning shortly to feel Barbara straddling my chest and staring directly at me. Her face must have been about six inches from mine. The expression on her face was cold and resolute. I was jolted awake.

I asked, "What's wrong." She replied, "I want a divorce." I was speechless for a few moments as she continued to stare at me. I asked, "What are you talking about?" She said, "I will always love you, but I am no longer in love with you and am moving to Saratoga Springs, NY, with Fern. I am in love with her." Fern was her lover and closest female friend. She had found a new home in Saratoga Springs, New York. "We are going to have our own new-age store in Saratoga Springs and will be living together. I will be taking Kristi with me."

My initial reaction was total disbelief. Was I dreaming? Could this be true? What spawned this sudden announcement? My head was spinning. I could hardly breathe. I grabbed her by her arms and pushed her away from me so I could get up. When I did, I was shaking. I demanded to know what had prompted this. She was utterly stoic.

I fell to my knees and implored her not to do this. She was intransigent. My mind reeled. How can I stop her from doing this? I told her we needed to talk. She said, "There is nothing to talk about. I'm leaving."

I tried for the next two weeks to find a way to persuade her to reconsider. She would not. My tears would not end for over a month. I began to think about how I could salvage our marriage. She did not want me to discuss this with our daughter, Kristi. But I knew Kristi suspected that something was not right with our marriage and that Fern had assumed a different role in her mother's life. I could see it in Kristi's eyes.

For the first time in my life, I felt totally powerless. My head reeled with thoughts of calling an attorney to press charges because they wanted to take my fourteen-year-old daughter out of state without my permission. I wrestled with how to tell David. Barbara insisted that I should not inform him until after the wedding when he had returned to Phoenix because she did not want to 'ruin his wedding. So, I acted as if nothing was wrong. I felt impotent to act. I was in denial and did not want to face the reality of what was to come. I felt like an outsider in my own marriage. I hoped that Barbara would change her mind and decide not to move to Saratoga Springs with Fern. This was the lowest point in my life, or so I incorrectly thought.

True to his word, David returned from Basic Training to marry Janey. They had a small, private wedding in the Westborough Congregational Church. Only a few relatives, friends, and guests were invited. Janey's parents held a reception at the local VFW hall. Janey's parents rightfully wanted to have a lovely wedding for their daughter, but their resources would not permit it. There was nothing memorable about it. They might as well have been married by the Justice of Peace.

David and Janey left immediately after the wedding to begin their life together in Phoenix. They couldn't wait to be on their own.

During the next few weeks, I continued to live in the house with Kristi, Barbara, and Fern. I thought that maybe a cooling down period would occur and that Barbara would reconsider. This was a delusional thought. Barbara and Fern moved to Saratoga Springs a few weeks later. There was no discussion possible about where Kristi would live. I felt powerless to stop them from taking Kristi with them. I could not stand the thought of watching them leave, so I escaped to a hotel in Newport, RI. They were gone when I returned.

The house was empty except for my personal belongings, bedroom furniture, some pots and pans, eating utensils, and a few plates and bowls. An ice pick was stabbed into a kitchen cabinet and had a note stating their new address. I never had the opportunity to say goodbye to Kristi. She must have thought that I didn't care.

I kept my promise not to tell David. I had become the betrayed husband, the victim, in my mind. It was one of the worst mistakes I had ever made in my life. My heart would never heal from my inaction to stop it from happening. I know that both David and Kristi would never understand why I didn't fight for my rights. But, in some perverse way, I felt relieved that

Barbara had taken Kristi with her. I knew that I did not have the skills to raise Kristi, a teenager, on my own, primarily because she was devoted to her mother. Barbara had a deep admiration for Fern's feminist bravado over leaving the Catholic convent where she was a nun.

David's mother finally told David on the telephone a few months later that she was divorcing me and living with Fern in Saratoga Springs. When he asked about his sister, she said that she and Kristi would be living in Saratoga Springs with Fern where they were going to open a gift shop.

David was confused and angry that his mother had not told him this before his marriage. He knew that his mother admired Fern but was unaware of her sexual attraction to Fen. He had no idea that his mother was interested in starting a business with her. She told him that she did not tell him this before his marriage because she didn't want to ruin his wedding.

David called me and was angry at his mother and me for not telling him before they were married. "Why would she do this, Dad? I thought you and Mom had the perfect marriage? What is wrong with her, what's wrong with you? Why didn't you tell me about this? Why does she have to divorce you to have a bookshop? You are my Dad."

"David, I wanted to tell you, but your mother insisted that if anyone was going to tell you, it was she. She was the one who left me, and she felt it was her responsibility to tell you since it was her decision."

"Don't you have any balls," he asked. "Why were you afraid to tell me? What is going on? Why does she want to live with another woman? Is she a lesbian or something, Dad?" My only response was, "You should ask your mother that, David."

He knew I had evaded his questions. The tone of his voice told me that he felt I had abandoned him again. At that particular moment, I could tell that he had lost respect for me. He felt totally disempowered and irrelevant. My guts ached for him. Once again, I had abdicated my role as his father.

Kristi wanted nothing to do with me. She had become persuaded by her Mother and Fern that I did not really love her. Kristi felt totally unimportant in my eyes because I did not fight to keep her with me. I had provided all the confirmation bias she needed. She was too young then to realize that I could have taken legal action because her Mother had taken her out of state without my consent. I did not want her to be exposed to a court trial.

For all intents, the relationship that Kristi and I had was now destroyed. It would take years for it to even begin to heal.

It took David years to even discuss this with his Mother. She told him she was bi-sexual. I was afraid he would never accept her again. Eventually, he could be with her without criticizing or judging her. After his discharge from the Air Force, he and Janey moved to Saratoga Springs to be near his mother. David wanted to be near his mother, so he could better understand her lifestyle.

Six months later, Barbara filed for and received a divorce from me. I sold our house and split the proceeds with Barbara, and moved to downtown Worcester, MA.

In the 1980s, proclaiming to be a bi-sexual or homosexual was not a badge of honor. The mere thought of two people of the same gender engaging in sex was considered by many to be an aberration. The term 'gay' was not yet a part of the American lexicon, much less an accepted way of life. Many called people in love with someone of the same gender viewed them as 'perverted,' 'queer,' or as a 'faggot' or 'lezzie' and a host of other deplorable terms. This was especially true in the military. It was almost impossible for David to admit that his mother was a bi-sexual. It made him feel like his mother was weird, and he never knew it. He was hurt and felt alone now that he had parents who were no longer together.

To further confuse him, his sister, Kristi, in her teens, lived with his mother and Fern, and he felt she could be influenced by their lifestyle. He simply could not reconcile this, and his anger was evident in his voice and behavior.

David and I had many conversations in person and on the phone about his concerns. David was upset with his mother's choice. David could not imagine his mother having sex with another woman. The thought of it toyed with his mind. He could not understand what had led her to become a bi-sexual. He was worried that this lifestyle would influence his sister.

I observed that while he came to accept his mother's choice, he never reconciled himself with it. He was in a rage for years over this. I didn't know if he ever could understand same-sex love. I know that his use of drugs and alcohol accelerated to the degree that he seemed unable to function without using them.

His resilience would once again be tested. He felt he could no longer count on his parents, to be honest with him. He was in a rage— a rage he never reconciled.

It tormented him all his life.

Phoenix ▪ 1983

David and Janey were living in a small apartment, off-Base in Phoenix. He seemed to like his job as an administrative technician and was progressing nicely. I visited them in Tucson six months after they arrived there. They seemed to be getting along well as newlyweds, but I knew that they were still drinking and smoking pot. This was the 1980s, and booze and pot were a lifestyle for people their age. They did not drink or smoke while I was with them; David shared that he and Janey were both "party" animals when he was off duty. When I asked him how it would affect his job, he told me, "No problem… everyone in my unit parties and covers for each other". David told me they had figured out how to beat the random sobriety tests and drug testing. He was not worried about being penalized because the rules were so lax.

I knew from my experience in Vietnam that this was the case. Only the most egregious offenders of drugs and alcohol were penalized. I assumed that he knew what he was doing. I realized that there was absolutely nothing I could do except to encourage him to devote his free time to off-duty education to better prepare for the future. I sent him motivational tapes and books about achievement. He liked them and discussed them with me when we had phone conversations.

Alcohol and pot were more important to him despite any motivation books or tapes could provide. The Deception of Resilience had become the theme of his life.

The Marriage That Should Never Have Been

While David and Janey were adjusting to Air Force Life in Phoenix, I started to look for a new life that would fill the painful void I felt living alone in Westborough. Barbara and Kristi were gone and living in Saratoga Springs with Fern while I was working at the college. I felt home-alone.

My social calendar began to fill when word of my divorce was posted in the paper. My phone began to ring from women I had worked with at the college and who were eager to fill the sexual void in my life. After a few months of accepting their passion and kindness, I longed for a more permanent and caring relationship.

I met many advertising and marketing sales representatives as the director of advertising and marketing at the college. I became personal friends with Michael, a sales representative of the rock radio station I used for radio advertising. Michael worked with and knew many female radio sales reps and introduced me to Roz, his colleague.

Roz was a real socializer and a party-girl. She was immediately attracted to me because she thought we could become the hot new couple in Worcester. She knew that I could refer her to other business contacts I had developed in the community. We began to date and to attend events that were held by the businesspeople we knew. Our relationship began to take on a more profound dimension.

Roz had been divorced for a few years and was anxious to settle down. She knew I was ready to have a constant companion also. After selling my house in Westborough, we moved in together to a new condo building. It was located in an up-and-coming district of the town across from the Worcester Art Museum — providing lots of visibility to prominent business contacts.

Our relationship developed over the next year, and we decided to marry in 1986. During the first few years, we had many enjoyable times with each other. We enjoyed each other's children and family holidays. Roz won three cruises for her sales performance. We cruised to the Caribbean islands and booked a week at the Grand Lido resort in Jamaica. We had heated arguments every time we traveled. Roz was never happy unless she was the center of attraction. She demanded that waiters and cruise ship staff cater to her every whim. I bristled when she treated others like they must jump at her every demand. We seldom had more than a day or two without an argument about her demands. She had to be in total control of me and everyone she knew. I would not accept her demands, her need for constant attention, her need to be complimented about everything she did every single day. My temper was short with her, and I did not know how to cope with her demands.

Roz was dependent on weekly visits to her psychiatrist, who she depended on for over 25 years, including the years we were married. I don't ever recall Roz's obsessive-compulsive behavior improving. We found a respite from the disagreements we had in Vermont — it became our conflict resolution spot. I knew of a country inn called The Castle Inn. Michael and Cheryl owned and managed the Inn. Over time, Cheryl became Roz's confidant and Roz was able to share her marital problems with Cheryl. They bonded, but the peace we found at the Castle did not last long.

Despite the disagreements and my inability to jump at her every request, we decided to marry. We thought that marriage would bring us closer together. How could it? What were we thinking? Roz planned the wedding with the owner of the Castle Restaurant. It is located in Leicester, Massachusetts, a small town right outside of Worcester. Roz's children, Stuart and Liz, and my children, David and Kristi, attended the wedding along with about fifty friends and close business associates. Everyone seemed to enjoy the wedding, but neither Roz's children or mine could understand why we wanted to be married. They had been privy to our incessant dissatisfaction with each other over the years we spent together.

They asked that I not ask them how to handle it. They thought we were crazy. They were right.

David liked Roz and enjoyed many conversations with her. She was a good listener and knew how to keep others talking about themselves. We visited him in Saratoga Springs, and he would visit us occasionally. Kristi was in college and in denial that I had remarried. She felt Roz was not authentic and never really enjoyed being with her.

I became disgruntled with our relationship and had a difficult time dealing with Roz's obsessive-compulsive disorder. She was in weekly therapy with many therapists for over twenty years. Out of frustration and no one to talk to, I shared my frustration with Kristi and David. They both told me to quit complaining because they didn't want to hear about it and urged me to divorce her. I did not immediately take their advice because I felt guilty about the divorce from Barbara. I was determined to make this marriage work.

At one point, we decided that we should enter marriage counseling together. We made an appointment with a marriage counselor who was recommended to us. We had one visit with him. At the end of the session, he said in a very straightforward way, "your marriage is over—end it." His advice was spot on, and we disregarded it, hoping that somehow, we could salvage it. Roz said he was a quack. I knew he was right

I tried to understand why our problems seemed unsolvable and sought advice from two different therapists. The first one had the same recommendation as did the first therapist we saw together—your marriage is over — end it. I wanted to end the marriage and sought a female therapist's advice who worked with me for over six months. She gave me the tools I needed to come to the self-realization that I could end the marriage on peaceful terms with Roz. The key was to make her feel important by telling her that I wanted her to be happy for the rest of our life. We both continued to live in dissatisfaction with each other. We kept convincing ourselves that we could make our marriage work. Despite our best efforts, we found ourselves continually arguing about our dissatisfaction with each other. We continued to live in the same house, but both of us led separate lives for the most part, and during the last two years of the nineties, we were seeing other people.

The nineties would usher in a new decade and a new path for each of us.

Adjustment

David was discharged from the United States Air Force in 1987 and returned to civilian life as a lost and unfocused adult. He and Janey moved to Saratoga Springs, NY, because he wanted to be close to his mother. He had finally begun to understand his mother's lifestyle.

Barbara and Fern finally had their own little New Age store on Main Street. They turned it into a popular destination for people looking for something non-traditional. They called the store The Nest of the Snowy Owl because it was filled with unusual items that emphasized the Native American people's pure spirituality. However, the store did not exclusively feature Native American objects and art. This store was a big success until Fern died a few years later. She handled all of the receivables and payables and had no way to pay them. Barbara lost the store and the house they had built.

David and Janey rented an apartment in Saratoga Springs, and David started to work for UPS. Janey worked in a hairstyling salon on Main Street. Their original intent was to save enough money to purchase a home and live a real life in the real world.

There was an obstacle standing in their way. Janey missed her family in Massachusetts and wanted to move near them. David dreamed of having a business of his own. Their marriage was never on an even keel. I knew from talking with David that sometimes he was high on weed and alcohol. Janey was not a heavy drinker but enjoyed lighting up a joint with David. It was their way of having fun. Janey was lonesome for her friends and parents. She wanted to go to school to become a hairstylist. Julie did not like Saratoga Springs. They had tired of each other. But after many arguments about where they should live, they decided they should not continue their marriage. They had no children and had grown tired of each other since they had little in common in the first place. Their marriage was not based on love for each other — it served as an antidote to the pain they experienced from aborting their child. Now, they were healed. Nothing was standing in their way of parting. They divorced on May 4, 1990.

Janey moved back to Massachusetts to be with her family. David decided he would return to Central Massachusetts to be near me. I left the college over a pay dispute even though I had increased the college's revenue to over five million dollars. I immediately found more significant and better positions in the proprietary school field.

I was working as a sales manager for a technical school that had an office in Worcester. He knew that I was in sales and wanted to give selling a try. I had an opening for an admissions representative and encouraged David to join the sales team. David was an instant success because he had grown up listening to me talk about interviewing and screening students for college admission and trade schools. After completing a training program, he started to earn a good living by interviewing and enrolling new students.

I became concerned with his free time behavior. He missed the party life and sought out his former high school friends, who were potheads and drinkers. Mentally, he was back in high school.

PART IV

The Nineties

"The '90s were extremely diverse, almost like
a laboratory of the new century. There was much
experimenting around in politics, economics, gender,
and family structures, and fashion. There was a cloud
of possibilities that kept all of us dizzy."

JILL SANDER, AUTHOR

Gretchen ▪ 1990

After his divorce from Janey when he was living in Worcester, Massachusetts, David met Gretchen in 1990. They both worked at different offices of the technical school where David worked as an Admissions Representative. She was infatuated with David's charisma and positive energy. He was impressed with her good looks, intellect, and can do anything attitude. They made a dynamic team together. They both possessed an entrepreneurial spirit and wanted their own business. They married in December 1992.

During the years they were married, Gretchen kept David under control. She had completed high school and had a few college courses under her belt. Her strength was in her German heritage of discipline, accuracy, and planning. She had a positive attitude. Based on her can-do philosophy of if someone else can build it, design it, create it… so can I. No project was impossible for Gretchen. She would have been an outstanding engineer.

They read an article in Entrepreneur Magazine about a New Jersey training program that taught aspiring businesspeople how to set up their own mobile bumper repair business. This program combined some business aspects with technical training in repairing and painting automobile and truck bumpers. It was a turn-key program.

Graduates were able to start their own business servicing automotive dealerships. These dealerships could not afford to repair the dents, scratches, and light damage to their new car inventory. New and used cars were moved around the lots all day by salespeople and customers. Dealers could not sell these automobiles if they had bumper damage. It would cost the dealership more to have their own technicians repair it than to pay for a mobile team's repair. David and Gretchen fixed the damaged cars and trucks right on the dealer's lot in just a few hours, enabling the dealer to sell them the same day.

They completed two weeks of training in New Jersey and returned to Worcester, ready to go. They bought a van and equipped it, and approached dealerships with their service. David was responsible for developing the business; Gretchen managed the details and assisted with the repairs. Bingo, they won a few jobs and earned about $450 in their first week. Within two months, they were pulling down close to $2000.00 a week and quickly drove that to $4000 within a year. Their work was excellent. They were dependable and it seemed that automotive dealerships had an endless supply of vehicles that needed to be repaired.

When they tired of working outside on dealers' lots in the brutal New England winter weather, they moved to Florida. They found an unlimited opportunity in the Jacksonville area because of the sheer number of large dealerships with hundreds of cars and trucks with bumper damage. They could work outdoors year-round. They became the bumper repair knights in the white van.

Their work was excellent, and they were dependable. Within six months, they had a route established with four or five dealerships that they served one day each week. They literally created a gold mine for themselves… a business that was a cash cow.

Gretchen was adamant about David remaining clear of alcohol and marijuana. While they both would occasionally 'party,' Gretchen had the discipline to not make it part of their daily life. She knew David had a real problem, and when they moved to Jacksonville and purchased their own home, she made David stay clean. Her German temperament was not to be tested, and David knew it. He remained clear of drugs and alcohol. Their business and personal relationship soared for a few years. David was happier than I had ever seen him.

I visited them at their home on a five-acre lot, which they purchased, renovated, and landscaped themselves. I was very proud of their achievements. They had developed a business that produced an exceptional cash flow based on their hard work and focus on success. They purchased a boat, and David took up water-skiing. He was a natural with his strong arms and highly developed physique. Gretchen was a natural at driving the boat. We had a lot of fun during the visits I had with them.

At one point in the late '90s, Gretchen traveled to Germany to visit her relatives. David remained in Jacksonville to service their clients. When Gretchen arrived in Germany, David arrived at the nearest liquor store. He was eager to get lit up again. He continued to drink and smoke pot until she returned and saw that he had relapsed into drugs and alcohol. David had betrayed the promise he had made to Gretchen to remain drug and alcohol-free. Gretchen did not believe in forgiveness for betrayal.

David's betrayal and deception were the beginning of the end of their marriage and business partnership. They were divorced on November 2, 2001.

Gretchen purchased her own van, and they split some of the accounts. Eventually, she developed a few accounts of her own, but developing new business was not natural for her. David continued servicing his personal accounts, grew others, and eventually moved to an apartment in Jacksonville.

The Deception of Resilience had entered his life again. It was in Jacksonville that he was first introduced to the Grim Reaper.

The August Surprise

My Father was born on August 8, 1904. Eighty-six years later, on August 8., 1990, I had a massive heart attack. I was 47 and thought I was going to die on my Father's birthday. Thanks to the talented cardiac surgeons at the University of Massachusetts Medical Center in Worcester, MA, my life was saved.

Roz was my patient advocate for all intents. She made sure that I was treated well. Her compulsive personality kicked into high gear, and she picked up on every mistake anyone made. After heart surgery, the first meal was pork chops, mashed potatoes with gravy, and a vegetable. She went into overdrive and carried the meal back to the nurses' station. She demanded a heart-healthy diet for me, and I received them until I was discharged.

David drove from Saratoga Springs to Worcester to be with me. He walked into my hospital room and saw the jungle of drain tubes, IV's, my oxygen mask, and monitors everywhere he looked. He started to cry and almost fainted. He had to leave the room but returned later when I was more ambulatory. Roz assured him that I would be fine, and he spent a bit more time with me. He drove back to Saratoga Springs the next day.

Kristi was due to leave for London to spend her junior year of college in England. She spoke to me on the phone but had to catch a flight to London.

I was discharged from the hospital three days after surgery, before the Labor Day weekend. Roz's son, Stuart, drove from Connecticut to help Roz take me home and up the stairs to our townhouse. He was supportive and sympathetic toward me and was a big help in getting me in bed and settled at home. I have never forgotten the kindness he showed toward me.

Part of the rehabilitation program at UMass was a twelve-week program of stretching and exercise, and meditation. It was an experimental program that measured recovery rates for those cardiac patients and those who did not. This program was a success and became a model for cardiac rehab programs throughout the nation.

Cardiac rehabilitation was a twelve-week exercise and meditation program at the hospital with walking exercises at home. The first day I walked was limited to one-minute walking outside, followed by one-minute to return home. The next week was two minutes, then three the next, etc., until I walked five minutes out and five minutes back. Roz found a brochure about the Boston Marathon Jimmy Fund Walk to raise money for the Dana Farber Cancer Institute kids. The Boston Marathon route was sanctioned and copyrighted by the Boston Athletic Club. The Jimmy Fund is the only organization authorized to walk on the BostonMarathon route, which begins in Hopkinton, MA, and finishes in Boston at Copley Square.

I registered for my first walk in September 1991 and walked the entire route for 15 years to help raise money for the kids. Each Marathon's training schedule required me to walk four miles a day, at least five days a week, throughout the year. In July and August, I walked on the weekends with an increasingly greater number of miles each week. By the end of August, I was walking sixteen miles on Saturday and twenty-two miles on Saturday of the week before the Marathon. I was in excellent condition before each week.

David joined me frequently on these walks. Kristi and her husband, Bob, walked with me one year without listening to my advice to condition for the walk for two months prior. Bob endured the Marathon with severe blisters on his feet. He crossed the finish line in severe pain and was treated in the emergency tent at Copley Square. He could not work for two weeks. Kristi was determined to finish with me while walking the final three miles, crossed the finish line, and fainted. She was treated for heatstroke at the emergency tent at Copley Square, the walk's terminus. Kristi, Bob, and I each proudly accepted the medal as we individually crossed the finish line.

Our hope that our marriage might survive seemed logical since Roz was such constant support and an enthusiastic cheerleader for my completed walks. But, that was not able to hold us together. Within a week after each Marathon, we returned to the confrontational behavior that we could not get beyond.

PART V

The 2000s

*"We must be willing to get rid of
the life we've planned,
to have the life that is waiting for us.
The old skin has to be shed
before the new one can come."*

JOSEPH CAMPBELL

A Time of Conflict

The Deception of Resilience became very pronounced in 2001 and 2002 when David lived in Florida alone after Gretchen's divorce. For the first time in a decade, he was entirely on his own and could eagerly continue to drink and smoke weed with no one looking over his shoulder.

He continued to work from his mobile van at auto dealerships, repairing bumper damage to the cars on their massive lots. He was extraordinarily talented and earned enough money to live exceptionally well. But he was lonely and missed the companionship of Gretchen. His resilience to alcohol and drugs' effects continued to build his confidence to feel he had himself under control. He continued to deceive him by descending into a quagmire of getting drunk, bouncing back as if nothing happened, and running a business with clarity and precision.

David's life up to this point had been a tortured one, it seems. He seamlessly rebounded from his first and second marriages. He was only deceiving himself into thinking that he could control any situation thrown his way. He harbored a sense of abandonment and loneliness that reinforced his need to connect with the only people with whom he could feel significant — addicts and alcoholics. He never thought that he would soon meet the Grim Reaper.

David rented an apartment in Jacksonville, Florida, following his divorce from Gretchen. His own mobile business was doing ok, but his alcohol and drug use were full-blown.

I visited him in July of 2001 to celebrate his birthday with him. He was eager to take me to the auto dealerships he had developed as clients and introduced me to his friends. One evening he told me he needed to have a little fun and was going out to a club so he could meet some women. He said he would return around midnight. He didn't.

David did not respond to my calls to his cell phone. I had no idea what club he had visited or what to do except to wait. I hoped that he had met a girl and was spending the night with her. I was afraid because I did not know.

He finally called me late the next morning to inform me that he was in the hospital and had been arrested and needed me to post bail before they would release him. I learned that he had been found in a dumpster by a man walking his dog and alerted him that something was wrong. His dog led him to the dumpster, and the man found David inside, seemingly dead. He called 911,

The police arrived, and an ambulance took David to the hospital. He had been beaten up and was unconscious. Apparently, David had made a move onto a couple of girls at the club. Their boyfriends waited until David left the club in a drunken stupor and beat him up severely, and dumped him in the dumpster, like a piece of garbage.

As he was recovering in the hospital a few days later, he became hostile due to alcohol and drug withdrawal. He physically attacked a male nurse who called the police. They took him to jail, and I bailed him out a few days later and drove him to his apartment.

I phoned David's mother in the interim, and she and his grandmother flew to Jacksonville. They were in his apartment when I brought him home from the hospital.

It was not a joyful reunion. Barbara and her mother were in a state of bewilderment. It seemed to me that they had their heads in the sand and could not face reality, nor could they acknowledge more than that David was beaten up at a nightclub. They left after a day or two and returned to their homes in Saratoga Springs, NY. They were in total denial of his addiction.

I hired a highly recommended attorney to represent David in court because he had been charged with assault on a hospital worker and a policeman. The attorney knew precisely how to get the charges dismissed. David was not charged with a felony.

David's attitude was that I had spent my money for nothing. He repaid the $5000 attorney fee. He had absolutely no remorse or appreciation for not being charged with a felony, coupled with a jail sentence.

The Grim Reaper had made his first appearance in David's life. He felt that his resilience was fortified again.

Claudia ▪ 2001

I rented a townhouse in Northborough, Massachusetts, after I left Roz. It was a perfect place to learn about being single again. I enjoyed entertaining women I knew who were interested in having dinner with a divorced guy who had spent most of his life as a married man. Perhaps they felt that my life-experience would add a different touch to their repertoire of tricks, and I was more than happy to accommodate them.

Four months later, the 9-11 terrorist attack on New York City blew in like a cold wind from the Arctic. 2977 people died, including the passengers on aircraft that struck the World Trade Center, the Pentagon, and in a field in Stony Creek Township, PA. It was difficult to believe that it was happening, and not some sickly produced interruption to the existing television schedule. After weeks of non-stop news coverage, America began to regain its bearings. Life slowly returned to a new normal.

My new normal turned out to be a new website, Match.com. That is how I found Claudia, a beautiful Brazilian artist who lived in Worcester. I sent her an email and mentioned that I understood the artistic temperament because my father was an artist. We exchanged emails for a while and agreed to meet at the Borders Book Store in Shrewsbury, MA. We really hit it off. A few days later we went out for dinner and planned to hike the Mid-State Trail. This 92-mile scenic trail runs from Rhode Island, through central Massachusetts, and north to the New Hampshire border. After the first walk up to the peak of one of the mountains on the trail, I knew that I had found my life-partner—something I had never experienced. A month or so later, Claudia moved in with me. She knew that I had separated from Roz and would file for divorce. Roz had already found a new housemate. Nothing was standing in the way of Claudia and my relationship.

I was very eager to have Claudia meet David and Kristi, so we visited both of them, and they came to visit us when they could. David was immediately fascinated with Claudia and the stories she told him about life in Brazil. Kristi was initially not as outgoing, but as the years progressed, she skeptically began to appreciate Claudia as totally different from Roz or her mother.

Claudia and I spent Christmas 2001 in New York City at the five-star Regent Hotel, where Kristi worked as an event planner. It was weird being in the Big City on Christmas Day. The streets were deserted, and restaurants were closed. We found a take-out deli that was open and enjoyed lunch on a park bench, while pigeons flew about us and pecked around looking for crumbs. We enjoyed hamburgers from room service at the hotel for dinner. They were delicious and worth every penny of the $38.00 charge for each.

We returned to my townhouse in Northborough after a day of touring the city. Claudia and I were now officially living together, and we planned to get married. I was eager to meet her two daughters in her hometown of Recife, Brazil, and meet her brothers and sisters. We flew to Brazil in May of 2002.

A day or two after we arrived, Claudia's brother-in-law, Roberto, invited us to join him and Claudia's sister, Rosa, on the archipelago of Fernando de Noronha. It is part of the Brazilian State of Pernambuco. It is the largest island in the archipelago and is 350 miles off-shore Recife. Our flight from Recife to the Island took ninety minutes. (Air France Flight 447 crashed off-shore Fernando de Noronha on June 1, 2009.)

Fernando de Noronha is breathtakingly beautiful. It is renowned for its undeveloped beaches and is a scuba diving and snorkeling enthusiast's dream. Gasoline-powered vehicles are prohibited, and all visitors must pay an ecology fee each day of their visit.

Roberto was the Governor of the Island for two years. He had done a fantastic job of making life easier for the residents of the Island. Roberto was honored in a public celebration in appreciation of his service. Afterward, we attended many parties at various restaurants and homes. Roberto was touched by the recognition and honor he received.

We returned to Recife a day or so after the celebration. We spent another week with Claudia's daughters, Nicole and Monique. Both of them were attending the University of Pernambuco in Recife. Claudia's relationship with them is the most honest and loving mother-daughter relationship I have seen. I knew they were going to be fine women, mothers, and marriage partners someday. We returned to Boston and took a limo to our home in Northborough. We were anxious for Christmas to arrive to spend it with Claudia's family in Recife.

December 2002 seemed to arrive quickly. We flew to Miami, and David met us at the airport. He drove us to his apartment in Naples so that we could spend a few days with him. David was anxious for us to meet his new paramour, Jamey. After spending a few days with him in Naples, he drove us to Miami, where Claudia boarded a Brazil flight. I had to return to Boston to work with my clients until Christmas week. I would rejoin Claudia and her family in Recife for Christmas. I flew to Recife from Boston two weeks later.

We had a wonderful Christmas with Claudia's daughters and her brothers and sister. It was fun to spend some time with all of them to get to know them better. I quickly learned to appreciate the Brazilian culture and music. Everyone welcomed me. The New Year's Eve party was a series of parties at Claudia's friends and relatives' homes. Claudia and I attended many parties on New Years' Eve. The most memorable was on the rooftop patio of an apartment building. We danced for hours to Bossa Nova music while enjoying the most fantastic buffet dishes of shrimp, lobster, roast beef, and desserts.

The day of departure arrived too soon. Claudia and her daughters were understandably emotional. An entourage of Claudia's entire family accompanied us to the airport.

Our arrival in Miami after the New Year Celebration in 2002 turned out to be the most dreadful of my life.

The Longest Day ▪ 2003

We were on different flights when we returned from Recife to Miami. Both flights departed within 10 minutes of each other, and both were direct flights to Miami. My plane landed first. I cleared Immigration and Customs and waited for Claudia's flight to arrive. I was expecting her to stroll into the baggage claim at any moment. That moment never came.

American Airlines told me that her flight had arrived but that she had not cleared Immigration and Customs. I knew that foreign passengers had a much longer line than U.S. Citizens and waited patiently. Miami International Airport is the gateway to the United States for travelers from South America and usually packed with arriving passengers trying to process through Immigration. A half-hour turned into three. Three became six. I continued to stand at the baggage pick up area, where she would pick up her luggage. Finally, after almost seven hours of waiting, I went to the airline agent's counter once again. I learned that Claudia was denied entrance to the United States. Customs put her on a return flight to Brazil at midnight. She was been removed from the United States because she had a tourist visa and previously worked in the United States.

Claudia would not be able to return to the U.S. for at least five years, when she could apply for a new visa. I would have to fly to Brazil to marry her. She could then apply for a Green Card to return to the United States.

U.S. Immigration had taken the woman I truly loved away from me. I was in shock and tears. Claudia was on a flight to Recife. I called David. He was still living in Naples in an apartment. I told him I was on my way to his apartment in a rental car.

The two- hour drive to Naples seemed to be a blur in time. I stopped at every rest area to regain my composure from crying torrents of tears and update him on my progress. I was in more mental pain than I had ever experienced in my life. As I arrived in the parking spot at David's apartment, he ran out and yelled, "Dad, Claudia is on the phone." I ran up the steps into

David's apartment and listened as Claudia told me that she was on a flight to Recife that would depart at midnight. She said that she was confined in the Immigration detention area. During the interrogation, the Immigration Agent said, "I am an Officer of the United States of America. You have no rights and are required to answer my questions. Do you understand that?"

They gave her one bottle of water, a cot, and a blanket after an intense interrogation. Sixteen hours later, an Immigrations Agent escorted her to a flight to Recife. She gave Claudia's Brazilian passport and other documents to the Purser on the aircraft. They would return her documents when she arrived at Recife.

Claudia was allowed one phone call. She called the Brazilian Embassy in Miami. They set up a three-way call to David's number — a brilliant move on Claudia's part. I told her I loved her with all my heart and would be back to get her no matter how long it took and asked her to wait for me to do whatever I needed to do to return her to my arms in the United States. She said she would wait for me and knew that I would return. It would be a two-year wait.

A New Mission

David was comforting and understood my emotional breakdown when he heard Claudia's phone conversation with me. He and I both knew that I would have a complicated challenge to bring Claudia into the United States again. He let me know that he would do anything he could to help us. There was no doubt in my mind that David was concerned and wanted to help us.

David drove me to the airport the next day for my return flight to Boston. I contacted my personal attorney, who referred me to a Boston Immigration Attorney. I made an appointment with him. He told me it might take three to five years for her to be admitted to the United States again. However, he proudly told me that since he was the president of a Massachusetts Immigration Attorney Association, he could hasten the process… for $5000.00.

I agreed to his contract with me. He immediately had his paralegal assistant prepare all of the forms and paperwork needed. I received nothing except obfuscation after many phone conversations about our case with this paralegal during the next six months.

I contacted my Congressional Representative, Jim McGovern. His assistant arranged a meeting to discuss how McGovern could assist me. The Congressman agreed to write a Congressional Inquiry into the progress of the paperwork. He provided letters from him to present to the U.S. Embassy in Rio de Janeiro to use when Claudia would have to be present for an interview there.

Claudia had a personal friend who worked at the U.S. Embassy in Recife, who helped her obtain an appointment at the American Embassy in Rio. She learned that I could easily submit the paperwork the esteemed attorney should have completed… I had paid for something I could have done myself. I fired the attorney, and Claudia and I each submitted the paperwork needed to keep the ball rolling. However, we knew it would be at least two years until we would work through the entire process.

In the interim, I arranged my professional schedule to visit Claudia frequently during the two-year wait. We were able to spend time together every other month or so. These visits presented an opportunity to form a closer relationship with Claudia's daughters and Claudia's extended family. These trips to Brazil allowed me to get to know Claudia's daughters much better.

Claudia took three round trip airline flights of 1150 miles each way-from Recife to the U.S. Embassy in Rio to submit her fingerprints that they kept losing. The American Embassy in her hometown, Recife, could not take fingerprints, causing her to incur expenses that could have been avoided. At times it felt that the process was never-ending.

The Immigration Process required that Claudia have a Permanent Resident Card — a Green Card — to reenter the United States. The card could be issued only if we were married. I flew to Brazil in March 2003 to marry Claudia.

Claudia and I were married on March 13, 2003, in a formal marriage ceremony at the Forum Rodolfo Aureliano, the Courthouse in Recife. Claudia's sister, Rosa, and Claudia's daughters, Nicole, and Monique accompanied us. This courthouse is a modern, beautiful building with an auditorium of stunning red walls. It can hold more than a hundred people. Twenty couples were waiting to get married. The Presiding Judge began the ceremony by reading in both English and Portuguese the history of marriage in Brazil. The laws are precise about the rights of the wife in Brazil, who have absolute equality in Brazil. The married couple must choose one of three pre-nuptial agreements that govern the disposition of assets should the couple request a divorce in the future. The first choice is Total Separation. Each spouse agrees that whatever assets they had before marriage is theirs to keep, as well as assets individually acquired after marriage. The second option is Partial Separation, which lets each party retain whatever assets they had before marriage, and that assets acquired after marriage are jointly owned. The third choice is called Total Junction, in which all assets they own are to be split equally.

Each couple then appeared before the Judge and asserted which option they chose and, after a few more words of counsel from the Judge, were pronounced man and wife. I was pleasantly surprised that the Judge spoke to me in fluent English and asked me a few questions about my perception of Brazil and of the United States.

Immediately after the wedding, Rosa took all of us out for lunch at a fine restaurant. Afterward, Rosa dropped us off at the apartment we rented to celebrate our marriage privately.

Our apartment had a private dining room that could accommodate seventy-five guests. Claudia had coordinated with the event manager and planned our wedding reception for Friday night, two days after we were married.

The reception was warm and happy. We invited fifty guests, and they all attended. The guest list included Claudia's daughters, Nicole and Monique, her sister Rosa and her husband Robert, and their son, Paulino and his girlfriend, Claudia's brothers and their wives, Claudia's closest personal friends, and family friends. This reception was full of energy and happiness. I was asked to make a speech and shared a bit of humor when I elaborated about how Claudia and I fell in love on a mountain trail that put us above the clouds. Fortunately, one of Claudia's friends spoke English and volunteered to translate my remarks.

It was heartwarming to see so many of Claudia's family and friends really enjoying themselves. I enjoyed getting to know them better. I felt more welcome than at any large event I ever attended previously. The reception ended around midnight. It was gratifying to see the guests commenting on how much they enjoyed our reception. Our hearts were full.

The next week was full of activity visiting relatives and preparing for my return to Boston. Claudia and the family accompanied me to the airport when I departed on March 19, 2003.

We played a waiting game for the next two years but made the most of it. I flew to Brazil to be with Claudia at least twelve times while waiting for the two years to pass. These trips were from two or three days to a month. They became extended honeymoons. We toured throughout the

State of Pernambuco and stayed at many fine world-class resorts. Each resort had its own style. There were hotels on the beach and others that were upscale bungalows that ensured maximum privacy. All of them had mammoth pools that meandered through the property and ultimately led to their well-manicured and private beaches. Most of these properties were staffed by Portuguese and English speaking employees. Since Claudia was a Brazilian, she communicated in Portuguese, ensuring excellent service.

The two-year wait passed much quicker because of these frequent trips to be with Claudia. We received notice from the American Embassy in Rio de Janeiro that Claudia would receive a date to receive Green Card and ensure re-entry to the United States. She flew to Rio and waited for me to join her at her hotel. My flight from Boston was delayed for a day and a half because of a snowstorm that paralyzed the entire east coast of the U.S. Now there was no time to spare.

Further delays would jeopardize our appointment at the American Embassy. Finally, the weather broke. I flew to Sao Paulo, transferred planes to Rio, and arrived at her hotel in Rio with just fifteen minutes to spare for our Embassy appointment. We walked into the Embassy and were the first people called that day. It seemed as if the sun was shining on us again. After we visited the Embassy, we had lunch, walked around downtown Rio for a couple of hours, and took a cab to the airport for a 10:00 PM flight to Boston together. It was 2005. Our life together became a reality after two years of wondering when we would be permanently together again.

Starting Over

After being visited by the Grim Reaper in Jacksonville, David continued to work at auto dealership lots painting bumps and scratches of new car dings and dents. Without Gretchen's support, he went it alone but occasionally bumped into her when working on her own automotive dealer accounts. She often called on David for sales support, but they did not re-establish their personal relationship.

Alcohol continued to plague him but not as severely as it eventually would. He seemed to want to be rid of both alcohol and drugs. David attended a few Alcoholics Anonymous meetings, although not on any frequent basis. His business provided sufficient income to let him live well and allowed him to immerse himself in a new idea or interest. It would consume his attention until he was bored with it. Then, it would be over, and he would never think about it again.

During these years of living by himself in Florida, we maintained a meaningful father-son relationship. I visited him frequently where ever he was. David and I relished our relationship. It was filled with laughter and discussions of the many things that interested him, including boating, hiking, astronomy, technology, the Illuminati, and extraterrestrial aliens. We shared the same bizarre sense of humor and could read each other like a book. He was passionate about these things, and I admired his in-depth interest and well-researched knowledge. He looked to me for advice on his business and always wanted my opinion of his ideas. He capitalized on my sales experience to improve his business. There was never any doubt the father-son bond we had established was strong. We loved each other.

David lived at a variety of locations in the Jacksonville area. His need to move frequently seemed to be based on his need to always have new female relationships to feel fulfilled. He docked the boat that he retained as part of the divorce settlement with Gretchen at a Marina and lived on it for almost a year. He said the boat was a 'chick-magnet' and had overnight company frequently. Other boat owners in the marina told him they enjoyed watching his boat rhythmically rock late at night.

Finally, he grew tired of one night stands. He missed the meaningful relationship he had with Gretchen and grew tired of working outside on the hot concrete parking lots of the dealerships, unprotected in the Florida sun in the summer and autumn. And then he met Jamie. She lived in Naples but was visiting friends at the marina and quickly became infatuated with David. He was entranced by her sex appeal and her ability to seduce him. Finally, he moved there and rented an apartment.

David was an expert at developing new business from auto dealerships. Soon he became the bumper repair vendor of choice for dealerships in Naples. He used his increased income to shower Jamie with gifts. She loved the attention he lavished on her.

It ended abruptly after almost a year when his drinking and pot use started to dominate their relationship. He began to drink heavily and smoked pot every day. Jamie was not addicted to alcohol or drugs. She soon tired of David's love of liquor and his diminished sexual drive when he was binging. It was impossible to live with or be around him when he was abusing, and she finally threw him out. David's resilience once again enabled him to accept her rejection.

David closed his bumper repair business there he decided that he had enough of Florida. He moved to Central Massachusetts, where he could be close to me and re-establish the accounts he had developed years before.

Peter Pan

It was easy to love David. He was Peter Pan in so many respects. It was fun to be with him. His insatiable curiosity about science, nature, aliens, astronomy, the Internet, camping, and his 'interest du jour' coupled with his need to be with people and entertain them made him a fun guy. He had the fascination of a little boy who endeared himself to others, especially women.

David was a faithful Peter Pan. He latched onto a woman quickly, and if he liked her, he became obsessive about her. David was not promiscuous. He was a devoted lover and showered his girlfriends with gifts and with all his attention and energy. How could you not want to have David around when you became the entire focus of his life? When he made you feel like you were the most important person in his life? Women become addicted to David and his Peter Pan-like innocence, and when coupled with his sexual prowess, they craved him.

The longest relationship David had with a woman was with his second wife, Gretchen. Subsequent relationships lasted two to three years until they ended. David always had an excuse for why they ended, but I knew it was because he was in love with alcohol and drugs more than his girlfriends.

David exhibited the classic Peter Pan syndrome characteristics in his social life but not in his professional life. He was entirely responsible and an expert in the management of his business. He created successful automotive bumper repair businesses in Worcester, Jacksonville, and Naples and dominated the market.

Northborough

David had saved a considerable amount of money when he arrived in Northborough at our home after leaving Naples. Claudia and I welcomed him, but we quickly tired of his unpredictable temperament, coupled with his futile attempts to hide his alcohol and pot use. We were able to persuade him to once again attend Alcoholics Anonymous meetings. He said he did not like to be around real alcoholics because he was different from them. He felt he could control his love of alcohol and pot and stop at any time he wanted. But, he didn't really want to and started to exhibit abhorrent behavior. He would deliberately try to trick local police into thinking he was doing something wrong in an attempt to prove them wrong. On one occasion, he dressed up in an arctic survival gear suit that completely covered his head and face and walked through the retired police chief's yard. Obviously, he looked like he was up to no good, and a town police officer arrived on the scene. He told David to lean against the police cruiser and to take off his hood and produce identification. The officer backed off when David accused him of unlawful search and seizure.

David had successfully intimidated the officer and gloated in "showing these cops that they don't have as much authority as they think they have." He disrespected the police since his high school friend's father, a police officer, kept confiscated drugs in his home.

Episodes like this continued. We knew that David could not continue to live with us. We told him he would have to find an apartment if he intended to stay in Northborough because of his disruptive behavior. He was angry at us for asking him to leave. I helped him find an apartment in town.

The Appalachian Trail

David discovered a love of the outdoors and of solitude that he craved for the rest of his life. The Outward Bound experience made such a lasting impression that he decided to walk the Appalachian Trail from Maine to Georgia. He felt it would be a life-changing experience.

He prepared for this trip for three years before moving to Northborough with us. As was his habit when he was interested in something, he devoted his energy exclusively to preparing for this 'walk in the woods.' He researched everything about the walk. He dove into the most trivial details of the trail. He learned about others' experiences to gain a complete understanding of what the most excellent camping gear was, what tents were the best, the fine points of hiking and camping. In short, no one could have been better prepared or have more excellent camping gear than David. He was the Appalachian Trail (AT) Aficionado.

Departure day arrived in the summer. I drove David to the northern terminus of the trail at Mount Kahadin, Maine. David chose to walk south to arrive in the southern states during the autumn when temperatures were cooler. He was set to embark on a 2,190-mile nature walk from Maine to Springer Mountain in Georgia. I gave him a huge hug and a kiss, a few words of advice, and he set out to hike to the top of Mount Kahadin. I was prepared not to see him for four to six months, although we would maintain phone contact when he could call.

The call came about 48 hours later. David had hiked to the top of Mount Kahadin. to begin the trip southward. He decided to spend the night in his tent next to a guy his age who started with him. The next afternoon David called me to tell me that he began to walk that morning and severely sprained his ankle. He pulled his ACL ligament and could not continue. He contacted a park ranger who took him to a medical facility where they told him to stay off his foot for two or three weeks. The sprain was severe, and the ACL needed time to repair. He told me he would stay there until it healed and then continue onward toward Georgia. He returned to his tent to recuperate.

While recuperating from his ankle injury at Mt. Katahdin's base, Maine, David found great comfort from several new-found friends. They were two adult girls who were camping next to David's tent. Or so the story went as told by David.

One night he was sleeping in his tent and heard the girls talking in their tent. He waited until the next morning and hobbled over to meet them. They were sympathetic for him and provided him with his favorite pain-killers — alcohol and marijuana. He was in seventh heaven. Unfortunately, these two ladies had to leave the next day and to continue their journey on the trail.

But, just when he was suffering from his ankle injury the most, along came the forest ranger who had taken him to the medical facility where he had been treated. As David narrated to me months later, the ranger was roughly his age and extremely attractive. She said she was just checking up on David's condition. The ranger gave him a grand tour of the area and its flora and fauna. She cooked dinner for him and nurtured him with more than apple pie.

David phoned me to tell me that he had decided to try to continue walking the trail again. Then, nine days later, he showed up at our home in Northborough. The forest ranger friend drove him from Maine. He said that he could not walk with his injured knee, now in a brace, and decided to return to Northborough to recuperate.

It was difficult to differentiate whether he was exaggerating, telling the truth, or fabricating stories. But, one thing is known about his experience at Springer Mountain —he never returned there. He never mentioned wanting to walk the trail again. Never. He abandoned what he claimed was a life goal and continued embracing what he loved the most: alcohol and drugs.

The Aftermath of the Appalachian Trail

Despite his knee injury, David was well enough to seek additional female companionship in Northborough. He met Gina, a young woman who was a hairstylist, and formed a relationship with her. David consumed all of her free time. She was wild about him. His use of alcohol increased, and I finally told him that he had to seek professional help. He reacted by storming out of the door, only to return a few moments later. The next day he attended an Alcoholics Anonymous meeting with a friend of his. Then he presented me with an expensive Breitling wristwatch and gave Gina an opal necklace with matching earrings. He seemed to be apologizing for his behavior to convince us that he would quit drinking. He didn't.

Four days later, he asked me to drive him to Sturbridge, Massachusetts, to meet his uncle Martin. Martin drove from Saratoga Springs to take David to his mother's home. I drove back to Northborough alone. David spent a few days there with them. He wanted to surprise his mother and grandmother, whom he adored. He presented his mother with a Breitling watch and bought his grandmother a 56" widescreen television.

David returned to Northborough in a rental car and said he wanted to spend more time with me. He had terminated his lease on his apartment in Northborough. I told him that he could stay with me until Claudia returned from visiting her family in Brazil. David was irate and told me I was selfish. Ten days later, he left and flew to Jacksonville, FL to pick up his van. David returned to Northborough in his van and asked me if he could pitch a tent in our backyard. He said he had not decided if he wanted to live in Northborough or in Saratoga Springs. Claudia returned from Brazil while he was in Jacksonville and reluctantly agreed to let him stay with us.

He immediately began to openly drink again when I was at work. Finally, my next-door neighbors told me that he was out of control when I was at work. He had been urinating from the top of the second-floor deck while screaming nonsensically.

The Labor Day weekend passed uneventfully. David had a series of irrational arguments with Gina, who was five years younger than David. He was eager for female companionship and sex. He had not re-established a bumper repair business. He was living on his considerable savings, so he had enough money to entertain her. As he did with almost every woman he dated, he became deeply attached to her and enjoyed her company. She was living with her brother in an apartment. She never invited David to stay with her when her brother was gone. David could not accept her reasoning and was determined to overcome this obstacle.

On a whim, he purchased a diamond ring and asked her to marry him. His alcoholic mind and psychotic obsessiveness caused him to think that this was the solution. I don't know if she accepted his proposal, but I know that his behavior became more bizarre. At one point, Gina told him she was going on her yearly vacation to Bermuda with her best girlfriend. David was furious and could not understand why she had to go off with another woman for their yearly vacation to Bermuda. She left on vacation with her friend. Gina was relieved and wished him well.

David was in a rage over this and ascribed delusional motivations to his girlfriend's need to take a vacation. He told me she must be a lesbian who wanted to have orgies with her girlfriend in a secret location. David dealt with this by checking into a hotel alone and binged on alcohol.

The next day he ended his relationship with Gina. He told us he was going to Naples, Fl. to live with his former girlfriend, Jamie. Jamie flew to New England to meet him for a short vacation on Cape Cod before return-ing to Naples. David moved to there a week later to live again with Jamie and her teenage daughter, Amber.

I heard little from David during the next month until he called me to tell me that he wanted me to know that he only gave me the wristwatch to teach me a lesson about giving. Two days later, he called to apologize. I knew from the tone of his voice that he had an alcoholic breakdown.

During the four months he lived with Jamey, he lapsed into periods of irrationality, fantasizing about sexuality gone wild. He called me often to tell me that he had great sex with Jamie and that she couldn't get enough of him.

He fantasized about Jamie's daughter, Amber, who was in her late teens. He imagined that she would end up in adult movies at some point. Jamie was successful in her career, and David attributed it solely to her sexual appeal, not her sales ability. Jamie would find him in horrifying drunken states in which he was barely coherent. He verbally abused her. Nothing she could do was enough for him.

Jamie begged David to quit drinking and abusing drugs. He wanted to have more booze, more often. She would have none of it.

Finally, she told David to get out and never return. She was done with him.

The Saratoga Springs Years

David left Naples and returned to our home in Northborough to pick up his belongings and move to Saratoga Springs. He had permanently ruined his relationship with Jamie. Moving to Saratoga Springs was his only viable option because he knew he could not live with us. His mother and grandmother were thrilled that he would be living in Saratoga Springs. He had deleted most of his savings and wanted to open his own bumper repair shop. He knew his grandmother would loan him the money he needed. His Uncle Martin chipped in, and they leased a building in Saratoga Springs. It was ideal as a bumper repair shop and had a second floor converted into an apartment where he could live. He and Martin became partners in the business.

Martin was a talented builder and completed the renovations. David concentrated on marketing and sales. No one in Saratoga Springs had ever heard of a bumper repair shop, so David distributed windshield announcements for months on cars in the mall parking lot and throughout the town.

David quickly established a strong business presence on Google with his own website. Within the first three months, they were acquiring customers. David had an uncommon artistic talent with a spray gun. He presented finished work that was so good that customers could not remember where the original damage was located. His reputation for quality work at a very reasonable price gained traction.

Within six months, they were working on three or four cars a day. People would much rather pay $400-$600 to have their automotive bumper repaired within hours. They would pay $1200-$1500 at a body shop and wait a week or 10 days for their automobile to be ready.

Saratoga Springs was home to many wealthy people who had luxury automobiles that cost $100,000 — $300,000. David recognized an opportunity to repair more than bumpers. He began repairing dents, scratches, and minor bodywork. Luxury car owners learned of David's skill. They flocked to his shop with their Rolls Royces, Lamborghinis, Porches, Mercedes, and BMWs.

The business prospered for about eight years. David's alcoholism resulted in mood swings that were destructive and damaging to the business and their partnership. Martin decided to remove himself from the day to day operations of the shop. They made an agreement that allowed David to buy Martin out over the next year. Martin returned to his other entrepreneurial ventures in acquiring and renting apartments. David would sorely miss Martin's sound reasoning and administrative expertise.

David continued his pattern of wooing women and showering them with sex and gifts. David moved in and out of the homes of two women who were initially wild about him. Eventually, they tired of his bizarre behavior and bipolar moods. They asked him to leave. David always found some reason why he left them. He was clearly becoming more and more delusional.

When Martin left, David was solo in his own shop. He couldn't keep up with the business that flocked to his shop. David knew he needed assistance. He hired an extremely talented spray gun technician named Roger. They hit it off exceptionally well because Roger was addicted to cocaine and weed. David had found a new soul-mate who could help him double his income and with whom he could party after hours.

Roger had a magnetic draw on young, college-age women who hung around local bars looking for guys who had drugs. David let Roger use his second-floor apartment to have cocaine-induced sex orgies with women on a nightly basis. David was not interested in group sex. He found a new girlfriend who had a home in town. David moved in with her. Roger exhausted himself in the apartment above the shop with a parade of young women interested only in sex and cocaine.

Nevertheless, the shop's business soared with two skilled technicians. Thanks to Roger's talent, they attracted more complex paint repair jobs. But, Roger presented a much different challenge than David anticipated.

Roger was addicted to cocaine that he acquired through a network of drug dealers well known to the local police. On several occasions, Roger had run-ins with the police, lost his driver's license, was under scrutiny, and started to behave dangerously.

David decided that his role was to be Roger's big brother. He visited Roger's mother to find a strategy to help Roger. He counseled Roger and loaned him money when he needed to pay attorney fees or other living expenses. But Roger blew the money right up his nose.

Roger finally stole money from the shop to buy cocaine. David had no recourse except to fire him. David tried to keep things running smoothly, but the business volume had increased significantly, and David knew he had to hire someone to work with him.

Grandma June

There was one constant in David's life. His Grandma June adored him, and he showered her with love and affection. They were devoted to each other, and while she never depended on him, she knew that he would drop everything if she needed him to help her.

June moved to Saratoga Springs after the death of her husband in 1984. After attending to her estate, she sold her home for over 40 years. She moved to Saratoga Springs to be closer to her daughter, Barbara, and son, Martin. She was thrilled when David decided to leave Florida to move to Saratoga Springs after staying with us in Northborough.

June was a relatively small woman with a powerhouse mind. She was as bright as the North Star and had an astute political sense. June was the only person I know who accurately predicted the winner of every Presidential election. Her memory was legendary, and her advice was sound.

David visited his grandma many times each week and always surprised her with an unusual gift. He had always wanted to tour the far western United States and wanted to do it in style. He surprised her by inviting her to travel through Montana and Wyoming one summer. She was all for it. David purchased airline tickets and made reservations at the most luxurious five-star lodges he could find. He showed her the beauty of Yellowstone, Grand Teton National Park, Glacier National Park, and most of the historical sites along the way. He persuaded her to take a helicopter ride over the mountains and above many areas of overwhelming beauty. She was all in and never blinked an eye. It was the highlight of her life. David was a video enthusiast and memorialized the trip with videos and still photos that she loved to view.

During the time she lived in Saratoga Springs, she moved several times. David was her hero in his van. She wanted for nothing when David was around. David was the perfect Grandson and devoted more time and attention to her than anyone else in the family. They had a magical connection.

David's Angels

"There are Angels that help me, Dad. They are always with me and protect me when I need them the most. They have helped me out of all of the bad events in my life, and I know they will always be there to help me."

David told me this many times, mainly when he had just survived another injury, accident, alcoholic binge, or setback in his life. He believed in Angels and thought that he could survive any catastrophe he caused. David worked with reckless abandon and with a short temper when things did not go his way. He would rant and rave and throw objects at the wall when he became frustrated. The Apple Store and Best Buy became his favorite places to buy cell phones, computers, GPS devices, fax machines, and anything electronic. He knew that if he damaged them, he could convince the store manager that the damage was accidental. They would replace whatever it was that David had demolished. He told legendary stories about how he could persuade these stores' managers that the accident was unavoidable. David was a high-spending customer and felt that the manager should replace or repair his electronic devices at no or little cost to him. He was good at it.

He continued to taunt the police. Ironically, the cops who pulled him over for his driving violations brought their personal vehicles to him for repairs. David felt that these cops were his Angels, also.

He didn't realize that these Angels had become the channel for his resilience. He called them Angels. I always knew they represented the deception of his resilience.

The Woman He Loved

David fell in love very quickly. He lived with two different women in Saratoga at different times. He showered them with expensive gifts and did everything he could to take care of their financial and emotional needs. David could not stop drinking and made no effort to stop. They eventually tossed him out. They could not endure his addiction.

He wanted to take care of everyone. His heart was full of acceptance of others —his grandmother, his mother, his girlfriends, down and out guys he knew, and his customers. David was a relater who needed acceptance. He received as much joy out of knowing that people would accept him as he did from helping them. It motivated him.

The realization that he needed to be accepted by one woman unconditionally led him to fall deeply in love with a woman he met in Saratoga Springs. Sally recalled how they met and fell in love.

"We met through an accountant who called me on the morning of November 26, 2013, to inquire about my interest in doing David's bookkeeping. That afternoon, as I left my last appointment (earlier than usual), David called, and we talked for quite a while. Then I offered to swing by as I was still in town.

"I started his bookkeeping right there and then. The chemistry between us was strong, and it was the first time I'd experienced a conflict of interest.

Two weeks later, I was anxious about him contacting me for a date. When he did, I had a request for him— if you become available, please let me know. David was so excited he immediately made a date to go to dinner at the end of the week."

"Our dinner date was quite formal until the end when we found ourselves standing in the parking lot as our cars were at separate ends of it. We were saying goodnight. David suddenly stepped forward and hugged me and kissed me."

David had found the woman with whom he became deeply in love. Sally came to love him just as quickly. Together they were enraptured with each other.

It ended twenty-three months later.

The Soldiers

David and Sally's love affair seemed to be a stabilizing force in David's life. It seemed as if he had found a woman with whom he could be comfortable and who genuinely loved him. Most of their non-working hours were spent together at Sally's house except for David's occasional need to be by himself in his apartment above his bumper repair shop.

David's love of camping inspired him to set up a tent in Sally's backyard where he could camp out with her and her son whenever they wanted to join him. Mostly though, David slept alone in the backyard tent. David had vivid dreams when he slept. They often awakened him in a state of fear and terror. He shared this vision with me:

"The soldiers were here again. I could hear their heavy boots pounding on the wet ground. The rain did not stop them from coming to see me that night — as they had many nights before — to tell me they were with me again and would protect me from danger. They were American Revolutionary Soldiers who had successfully fought the British. This night was different, Dad. I could hear it in their voices as they waited for me to come out of the tent. When I did, the Captain put his hand on my shoulder and said, David… we will no longer protect you because you are not interested in saving yourself. I cannot ask my soldiers to put their energy to use by protecting you. There are too many who need our help and will use it to get better, but not you. You will not see us again; we are done with you."

The dream terrified David. Claudia and I could see the fear in his eyes when he shared this with us. We knew that something had changed and knew it was not for the better.

David tried to fight his way to sobriety and sanity for the next eighteen months. He scheduled visits with social workers for help. I urged him to schedule an appointment with a cognitive therapist who wrote prescriptions for psychotropic drugs instead of establishing a counseling regimen. David would take his medication as prescribed only when he felt he was having problems. He lied and told me that he was attending Alcoholics Anonymous meetings and his social workers and saw a psychiatrist. Sally told me that he was canceling his meetings or just refused to show up.

When I confronted him about this, he told me that these professionals were only after his money. Sally knew that David was in crisis but could not convince him that he needed to be admitted to a rehabilitation facility. His mother was afraid for him and drove by his bumper repair shop two or three times a day and parked across the street to see if he was functioning. Neither Sally nor his Mother clued me in on this, but I knew from his vocal tone when I spoke to him on the phone when he was drunk. His voice betrayed him with its exaggerated enthusiasm. Often, he would not answer the phone when I called. I persisted and finally reached him.

I urged him to drive to our home in Massachusetts to visit us because we would be moving to Florida within the next few months. When he arrived, we discussed his addiction. I told him, "If you continue the path you are on, David, I know one of two things will happen. You are going to kill yourself, David. You must stop all alcohol and drugs."

Fear gripped me. It was like I could see this happening vividly in my mind when I spoke those words to my son. I had tears streaming down my face as I dropped to my knees and pleaded, "David, promise me that you will never use drugs or drink even a sip of alcohol again… ever. I can't handle any more calls saying they found you passed out near death or that the paramedics were called to revive you. I can't take it anymore, David. I can't take it anymore. I'll do anything I can for you, but I can't take this."

I grabbed him by his legs while sobbing on my knees and pleaded, "Promise me, please quit drugs and alcohol. I know what is coming."

"I promise, Dad. I promise."

The Eye of Happiness and Joy ▪ 2015

David planned to visit us in February 2015. Instead, he went on a significant alcoholic binge resulting in his unconsciousness. He was discovered in his shop by his mother. He was taken to the hospital by medics, who said he would have died within an hour if she hadn't found him. This was one of many such episodes she had observed during the past year.

I knew he was not serious about sobriety. I told him I would welcome him to visit when he had been sober for six months, thinking that this would encourage him to stay dry. He promised that he would seek psychiatric help and would attend Alcoholics Anonymous daily. That promise, like all others he made over the past 25 years, was broken. He was broken more than he admitted.

I realized that a six-month without booze restriction was only contributing to my inability to be with him. This binge drinking had slowly increased in frequency and intensity. He seemed to be on an established twenty-eight-day pattern of being sober and then suddenly binging. Sally said the twenty-day pattern was like clockwork. She had reported such episodes to me previously, but now they were out of control.

David and I talked on the phone almost daily, and he seemed to be getting much better. Sally cautioned about the upcoming twenty-eighty day from the last binge. She had it pegged. He went through the Spring and Summer of 2015, increasingly more separated from the reality of his problem. The twenty-eight-day cycle continued, each one more severe than the other. She was frightened for him and did not know what to do.

I had become convinced that his addiction problem and psychological problems were soon going to render him incapacitated or that he would end up in jail. He continued to drink and drive, and in the Spring of 2015, he was in a drunken rage and hit a car parked in someone's yard. He fled the scene to his apartment above his bumper repair garage. When the police arrived on his premises to question him, David was drunk. He was resilient enough to tell the police they had no right to be on his premises and that he had been there all night. He told them there was no law against getting drunk on your own property and that they had no proof he had not been there all night. The police left. They did not inspect his vehicle for damage because it was in his garage, and they did not have a warrant to enter.

I was very troubled by David's drinking himself into unconsciousness, requiring EMT's to take him to the hospital, and then his refusal to follow his caregiver's instructions. His belligerence and defiance of the police and his attitude about drinking seemed to be getting worse. He was losing control.

I phoned his sister to determine if she was interested in joining me to seek a court order to have David committed for his safety and the safety of others. I anticipated that she would not because, like her mother, she would do anything to avoid confrontation. After thinking about this for a day or two, she told me she wasn't comfortable with it and didn't think it was necessary. I decided to put this idea on hold for a few days. I thought I would give him another chance.

In August, I invited David to visit with us in Orlando. He booked a flight to Orlando. Claudia and I were excited about this reunion because we had not been together with him since November 2014, a month before moving to Orlando.

We picked David up at the Orlando International Airport on September 30. Claudia and I were thrilled to see him. He was sporting a new short hairstyle, almost a buzz cut. He was totally lucid and conversational and was in excellent physical condition. His spirits were high, and we enjoyed spending the afternoon with him at Lake Nona. I gave him a tour of the new Medical City and the high tech businesses and housing areas that were part of the rapid development.

David seemed to be much improved. He looked terrific and seemed to be in complete control of himself. I was glad that I did not proceed with a plan to have him committed.

His attitude and appearance during this visit reflected someone who was in control of himself. It was a pleasure to have him with us. Sadly, he had fooled us into thinking he was in control of himself.

David feigned interest in our new apartment and the development of Lake Nona. I sensed that he was mentally in Saratoga and was itching to get back. He conducted business phone calls and checked in repeatedly with Sally. He seemed to be paying lip service to the plans we had to show him our new community and all it had to offer. I knew he had not arrived here mentally and sensed that he was eager to return to his best friends — Alcohol and Marijuana.

On October 1, 2015, the three of us drove to the Orlando Eye, the 400-ft. version of the London Eye, the fifth-largest Ferris Wheel in the world. This is not your typical Ferris Wheel because of its immense size and passenger capsules that can carry up to fifteen passengers. These all-glass capsules offer a breathtaking view of the entire Orlando area. One complete revolution took about 22 minutes.

David has always loved attractions like this and was all pumped up about riding in it. As was his style, he had researched all he could find about the Eye and was enthralled with it. The three of us stepped into a capsule and were on our way to a new experience. We were amazed at seeing the entire city of Orlando and 50 miles in every direction. We commented on the vast flatness of the land compared to New England's hills and mountains. David seemed to be thoroughly enjoying himself and seemed very happy.

The Eye is located right next to Madame Tussaud's Orlando Wax Attraction. David was intrigued by the authenticity of the characters. He wanted pictures of himself next to most of them. David was especially interested in Einstein, Steve Jobs, and Marilyn Monroe. He couldn't seem to get enough information about how the lifelike waxed characters were made. He quizzed each tour guide and employee he met about how someone could get a job crafting these celebrities. David was as happy at the Eye and at Madame Tussaud's as I had ever seen him.

Claudia was deeply touched by David's childlike curiosity and excitement with these characters and enjoyed having her picture taken with

David. She becomes very emotional every time we pass by the Eye when we are in Orlando. She had developed a genuine love for David's innocence and his caring-sharing personality. We hoped that he was on his way to recovery. This was one of the best experiences I ever had with my son.

The day that followed was the worst. We took David to Celebration, Florida. Celebration is a census-designated town and a master-planned community near Walt Disney World Resort. It had been built by Disney and was intended to be a prototype community of the future. It was often described as the too-perfect town of "The Stepford Wives" because of its unabashed neo-urbanism. In 2004 Disney sold most of its stake in Celebration to a property management company, but the Disney spirit lives on.

We had visited Celebration a month or so before David's arrival in September 2015 and found it to be really charming, a perfect place for those who crave regimentation and life as it was in the 1950s. It is lovely, beautiful, well-designed, and smacks of uniformity. It was as if Father Knows Best was the inspiration for the town. We found a seven-mile planned bike trail that enabled riders to see all of Celebration. Bicycles could be rented at the trailhead. We decided that since David loved to bicycle on trails, we would take him to Celebration for the day.

We drove to Celebration on October 2, 2015, and arrived 35 minutes after leaving Lake Nona. We immediately drove to the parking lot at the bike rental station. It was a beautiful autumn day in Orlando. The temperature was in the high 80's with Orlando's puffy white cumulus clouds meandering across the afternoon sky. David was excited about riding on the trail, which was outlined on the map we received. The 7-mile trail included riding on residential streets, boarded trails that crossed swampland, business development areas, and finally, through the Town Center before ending at the trailhead.

The weather forecast did not mention any storms at all. We encountered a non-weather related terrifying storm we could never have anticipated. It haunts me to this day and will never leave my memory.

As we biked on a sidewalk next to a major highway, I had to stop because I had a kink in my back. I asked David, who was riding next to me, to stop and crunch my back muscles while following Claudia, who had the bike trail map. We stopped, but Claudia kept riding because she did not know we had stopped. I told David to quickly ride his bike to tell her to stop and wait for us. Instead, he yelled, "Claudia… Claudia" to summons her. I told him that she would not hear him because of the traffic noise and the wind's direction.

She kept riding. David crunched my back and massaged my shoulders for a few minutes, and then we decided to ride on. Claudia was nowhere in sight. We continued to bike while looking for her. We could not find her. We had no idea where she was. I did not have my phone with me asked David to phone her, but he opted to continue to look for her. We rode for 20 minutes and could not find her. For some strange reason, he refused to phone her. Instead, he transformed into a madman.

David became confrontational and red-faced angry, and screamed at me. I stopped.

"Why wouldn't she stop? Why did she ride on? Couldn't she look back and see that we were no longer behind her? What the fuck is wrong with her?"

He was out of control so violently that I did not respond to him. There is no way to reason with anyone who is out of control. He was throwing things, screaming at me, and on the verge of striking me when Claudia appeared from behind us.

She had backtracked from where she thought she had last seen us and rode the entire trail again to finally find us. She was flabbergasted when she heard David screaming at me and stopped to help. I implored him to calm down. David would have none of it and was calling her everything from inconsiderate to being arrogant and uncaring. He rode away in a fit of anger, turned around two blocks later, and came back to scream some more. I was hesitant to step in to grab him because he was so entirely out of control. We just ignored him and rode toward the town center to reach the trailhead to return our bikes. He rode silently behind us until we arrived at the bike rental return.

By this time, David had cooled down a bit but still wanted to yell at me. After returning the bikes and walking toward our car, he blurted out to me:

"Why can't you admit that you are an addict?" You are never wrong, are you? You are addicted to drugs, to booze, and to sex, and you have been for years."

I said, "David, you are out of control and have no basis for accusing me of these things. I am addicted to nothing." Claudia told him straight out that he was delusional. It was clear to me that David had been influenced by his mother to blame me for his addiction. He was having a psychological crisis. He had been without alcohol for two and a half days and seemed as if he was crashing.

Claudia and I both were afraid of him. We didn't know what to do. We thought it best to head straight back to our home, hoping that the 35-minute ride in the car would calm him.

We drove back to Lake Nona in silence. David threatened to get out of the car and find a cab to take him to the airport while traveling at seventy miles per hour on an expressway. He talked about how he was not wanted in our home and that he would never return. He was still in a rage. We said nothing and drove to our home. The longer we drove, the more contrite he became.

We knew that David did not drink while he with us, but we had no idea whether he was still smoking weed during those short intervals when we were not together. He had told us that he had quit taking the psychological drugs that had been prescribed to him. He just stopped taking them without any guidance about how to wean himself from them. His conversations were jumbled and sometimes incoherent.

I told him he was not leaving that night and that I would take him to the airport in the morning for his scheduled flight back to Albany, NY.

Claudia prepared a delicious tuna kabob dinner for us, and David loved it. Dinner conversation was strained and uncomfortable.. We went to bed early. David watched TV a while and then went to the guest bedroom for the night. I know he didn't sleep well because I could hear him roaming about our apartment many times during the night. Claudia and I were emotionally exhausted.

It was a short night, and when I awoke the next morning I saw him sitting outside at the pond on the bench. He was deep in thought. My heart ached for him.

We had breakfast together, and he and Claudia and I made small talk. It was like everyone's heart was broken, and no one knew how to talk about it.

I drove David to the airport. Our conversation was limited. I urged him to quit drinking, quit smoking weed, and to seek additional help. Again, I told him that he would either end up in jail or in a casket from overdosing if he did not. I stopped at the terminal. He exited the car, grabbed his bag, and entered the terminal. I said to him, "Take care of yourself, David." Those were the last words I spoke to him.

Ever.

He grabbed his bag from the car and walked into the airport. I drove away.

He never looked back.

I was devastated. Did I do the right thing by just letting him get out of the car and fly to his home? Should I have gone inside the airport with him to hug him and kiss him goodbye? I wanted to tell him that I loved him and would do anything I could to help him, as I had done so many times before. Had I abandoned him again?

The Final Days ■ October 2015

David returned to Saratoga Springs from his visit with us in Orlando.

I did not speak to him again. He didn't call me, nor did I call him. It seemed as if there was absolutely nothing to say. It had all been said so many times before. That night Claudia found this note under her pillow:

10/3/15
Dear Father and Claudia,

This morning as I began to awaken, I was taken by a very
sick feeling. Memories of yesterday flashed thru my mind.
I was hoping it was merely a dream. My stomach began
to feel sick. Within seconds' reality set in! I had to face
my music… I lost control of myself again. I pray that one day
I can maintain a normal existence and control my emotions.

I am truly sorry for how I made both of you feel.
Please don't take it personally. I love both of you!

David

This was the last communication, written or verbal, that we received from David. We never heard from him again

David returned to his bumper repair shop and his apartment on the second floor of the shop.

David's girlfriend, Sally, knew that David had returned and was not himself. He told her that he had a lousy meltdown with Claudia and me, and she could tell he was deeply affected. As each day passed, he did not communicate with her. Sally was worried. He always phoned her several times a day. Now nothing. She called him but was only able to leave a voicemail.

Frank, David's helper, knew that David drank a bottle of vodka every morning and another every evening. Frank worked in the shop between 10 AM and 5 PM. He found David passed out in the shop before work began on many occasions over the previous few weeks. David recovered enough by 10 AM to work on cars and talk to customers. But he was working fewer and fewer hours each day. Jobs that should have been completed were delayed. Customers were beginning to get impatient. No one called me to tell me that David was drinking himself unconscious each day.

David's mother knew that he was not himself. She was used to him calling her each day, sometimes every other day. But she had not heard from him at all that week. She drove past his shop to see if he was working and sometimes parked across the street to see how he was. But, she did not approach him or try to figure out what was going on. She said she will never forgive herself for that.

On the 15th of October, 2015, David's coworker, Frank, came into the shop after his lunch break and found David on the shop floor. He had to revive David from unconsciousness. He helped carry David into his bed. He left David alone for the rest of the afternoon and did not re-open the shop. He notified no one. He checked on David later in the afternoon and found David assumedly asleep.

Later in the early evening, Frank checked on David again and smelled an unfamiliar odor. As he walked up the steps to the apartment, he discovered a fire simmering in the plastic shower stall, creating lots of acrid smoke and excessive black soot. He rushed to David's bedroom and found him lying on the floor covered with black soot. David appeared to be dead. Frank was beside himself. He called 911.

The fire department and police arrived, pronounced David dead, and transported David's body to the coroner. The police declared the shop to be a crime scene because they did not know what had happened and could only assume that there might have been foul play. David's uncle, Martin, became the point person because he and David had been partners at Saratoga Springs Bumper Repair

Martin informed David's Mother, and his sister, Kristi, called me.

I received the phone call that I had feared for years at 9:00 AM on Thursday, October 16, 2015.

"Dad... David's dead".

My daughter, Kristi, uttered only those words when I answered. I paused ...

"No, Kristi, no — tell me what you mean...why, how, when?"

Sobbing uncontrollably, she said, "There was a fire in his apartment. They found him, and he was dead."

I dropped to my knees. Claudia, my wife, ran into the room.

"What happened?"

I answered, "David is dead."

"Oh no, Oh, no!"

He would never again drink or use drugs. He was now permanently dead drunk.

Post-Mortem

Claudia and I were not surprised by Kristi's call. We knew that David was on a downward spiral. I thought he should be admitted to a rehab facility or that he would die from his addiction. I was angry at myself for not going to Saratoga Springs with him when he left us. Maybe, just maybe, I could have stayed with him and taken a pro-active role in talking to his social workers, psychiatrist, and his girlfriend Sally. Maybe I could have helped him when he was now unable to seek the right kind of help. There was no reason why I did not return to his shop and apartment. I was semi-retired and had no commitments that would have interfered.

I failed to make the most critical decision of my life… to help my only son save his own life. It still hurts me so deeply that my despair has turned into guilt.

My soul was wounded. I felt guilty that David might have given up on himself because he thought I had given up on him. I knew there would be a lifelong period of recovery for everyone he loved and who loved him. There simply were no words.

We waited 48 hours until we knew what would be the next step in the investigation into his death, the necessary funeral arrangements, and the disposition of his body. We flew from Orlando to Albany and then rented a car to Saratoga Springs. We met his sister and Kristi's husband, Robert, David's mother, and his Uncle Martin and his wife, Liz.

In the aftershock of this tragedy and the absolute necessity to make arrangements, Martin and Kristi were appointed the administrators of David's estate. David had died intestate, and almost all of his records were destroyed in the fire. Luckily, Martin was able to find most of his valuable personal records, financial records, and bills to be paid. Kristi's husband, Robert, a firefighter in New York City, helped Martin make sense of what was left of value in the apartment. They did not find much. They would not let me help them because Robert said it would be too difficult for me to observe, based on his experience with similar fires.

Kristi seemed to be in a state of shock. She had never wanted to associate with David because she disapproved of his lifestyle and his alcoholism. Now, Kristi was coping with her decision not to join me in having David committed to a rehabilitation facility. She did not want to be involved, and now she was staring at the remains of that decision.

Kristi, her mother, and I determined that we wanted David's body to be cremated. David's shop was next door to a funeral home. David had become close friends with the owner, Roland. He made it his mission to take care of David personally. Roland arranged for the cremation of David's body. He arranged a personal viewing for the family and a short three-hour visitation visit for friends and other relatives. We are incredibly grateful for the loving care he provided for David's body.

I volunteered to do the most emotional task I have ever had to do in my life. Claudia and I shopped for a shirt, sweater, and trousers that Roland would use to dress David's body in the casket. As I looked at clothes in the men's department of a clothing store, I found myself on the verge of physical and mental collapse. I pointed to some items for Claudia to purchase and had to leave the store to walk around the parking lot sobbing. All I could think of was, "I am buying clothes for my only son's funeral. I loved him with all my heart." I was unable to do anything to stop him from destroying himself through alcohol and drugs.

I wanted him back. I still do. I always will.

The Funeral Service

Roland Harris is the director of the Loving Care Funeral Home. He and David had become good friends because David's shop was next door to Roland's funeral home. Always the helpful guy and friend maker, David had formed a real bond with Roland and snowplowed Roland's driveway unannounced just to help Roland. Always inquisitive, David took a real interest in the operation of a funeral home and would ask Roland to show him around and explain the role of a funeral director. David loved to know how different businesses worked and what the owners had to do to make a living.

Roland arranged two services for David at his funeral home. The first was an evening "viewing" service for anyone who wished to attend. Claudia and I and David's mother and grandmother, David's sister and her husband, Robert and their two sons, Jake and Cole, his Uncle Martin and his wife, Liz, and David's cousins attended both services. David's girlfriend, Sally, attended also.

I had been to more funeral services than I would care to remember. Obviously, this was the most emotional one for me (and I am sure for everyone who loved David). Here we were welcoming people to view David's body, which Roland had meticulously prepared. As with every funeral, it was difficult for people to find the right words. In this case, words were cautiously used because it was unclear to many how David died. Some asked. Most did not. We explained that David died from smoke inhalation caused by a fire in his apartment. No one probed further. Some gave accounts of the last time they saw David. All were incredulous. Some were skeptical. All were sympathetic. This service lasted only about three hours.

A separate memorial service for the family was held the next afternoon. We all sat in a circle in the room where David's casket was located. I was asked to lead the service. I gave this eulogy:

"Our thanks and appreciation and love go out to each of you. We are gathered here to remember the life of David. I would ask you to offer one word that you most feel characterized David." These words were offered:

*Unique • Loving • Lover • Handsome • Contrarian • Caring
Strong • Opinionated • Helpful • Resilient • Creative
Entrepreneurial • Artistic • Great sense of Humor
Devoted to His Mother and Grandmother*

My Eulogy Continued...

"David was born in 1964 while I was stationed at Incirlik AB, Turkey. He was 10 months old when I met him. I left him again in 1968 when I was sent to Vietnam. I have always felt that David and his mother were casualties of that war, as were all of us. Children and wives were the unrecognized victims of the war. I don't think David ever got over the abandonment he felt when I left him.

"Together, he and his second wife started a mobile bumper repair business. After their marriage ended, David relocated to Saratoga Springs to be close to his mother and grandmother. With a loan from his grandmother, David and his uncle, Martin, opened Saratoga Springs Bumper Repair.

"Here is what David left every one of us with:

"Memories of a great man who suffered through his life because of alcohol and drug addiction."

"He let each of us know how much he loved and cared for us."

"He impressed us with his great curiosity and love of all he did. He confused us with contradictory stories about his activities as he tried to cope with his addiction without us knowing. But, we knew his intention was not to hurt us."

"He always expressed his love for us and regretted having hurt us with his bizarre alcohol and drug-induced behavior."

Most importantly, he lived his life his way and did it with gusto.

When he shall die
Cut him into little stars
And he shall make the
Face of heaven so fine
That all the world will
Love the Night
And Pay no Worship
To the Garish Sun.

WILLIAM SHAKESPEARE, ROMEO AND JULIET

"Tonight and every night for the rest of your life, look at the stars. David will be watching."

Irony

Everyone went out to dinner at a restaurant after the private service. It was perfunctory and indeed not a fun night for a family who had seldom been together in the previous thirty years. David's mother and sister could not stop crying. It seemed to me to be surreal.

The next day Martin's wife, Liz, prepared lunch for everyone that she served in the recreation room of David's grandmother's apartment building. It was a little more upbeat but not intimate. The next day, David's body was cremated.

Kristi's husband, Robert, had experience in navigating through the remains of a fire. Martin knew the building intimately and knew where David kept his personal possessions, records, and shop materials. They told me that they didn't want me to help them sort through David's possessions in his burned-out apartment. They felt that it would be too much of an emotional task for me. They wanted to take care of the clean-up and salvage operations by themselves. Matin and Kristi were appointed Administrators of his estate.

Claudia and I returned to Orlando.

David's mother was so grief-stricken that she could not stop crying for three months. She coped with her grief and guilt by drinking and had two automobile accidents. No charges were filed.

The garage that housed David's bumper repair business and the apartment where he died from smoke inhalation was renovated and turned into a smoke shop in the year that followed. They sold tobacco products, bongs, and smoking paraphernalia.

The owner of this smoke shop named it **Ex-hale.**

Epilogue

It rained all day and all night. It rained all day and all night for thirty-four days and thirty-four nights. Suddenly it stopped. A half-ton truck passed by on the dirt road I was walking. It kicked up dust. It was monsoon season in Pleiku, Vietnam 1968. The soil sucked in the rainwater as fast as the Viet Cong and we killed each other.

I was one of the fortunate ones. I would live through Vietnam and return to "the world" twelve months after arriving in Saigon.

Forty-six years later, I stared into a casket at the corpse of my only son, David. The dust from his cremation floats in a glass paperweight that resides on my desk, staring at me every day. It speaks, "Dust-to-Dust, Dad." He will not be returning to the real world. I often wonder why he is not the survivor instead of me.

I am haunted by survivor's guilt.

About the Author

Harrison Rider Greene is a nationally known
business consultant and has written extensively
about the Exciting Future of Sales.
He lives in Florida, with his wife, Claudia.
They love international travel.
This memoir is his first book.
Contact Harrison at **uniquehrg.com**